MOON
SIGNS

£6.00

D0319425

MOON SIGNS

Reveal your inner feelings
and discover your future

SASHA FENTON
& JONATHAN DEE

C&B

COLLINS & BROWN

First published in Great Britain in 2001
by Collins & Brown Limited
London House
Great Eastern Wharf
Parkgate Road
London SW11 4NQ

Copyright © Collins & Brown Limited, 2001
Text copyright © Sasha Fenton and Jonathan Dee, 2001
Illustrations copyright © Mandy Pritty, 2001

The rights of Sasha Fenton and Jonathan Dee to be identified as the
authors of this work have been asserted by them in accordance with
the Copyright, Designs and Patents Act, 1988.

All rights reserved. No part of this publication may be reproduced,
stored in a retrieval system, or transmitted in any form or by any
means, electronic, mechanical, photocopying, recording or otherwise,
without the prior written permission of the copyright owner.

1 3 5 7 9 8 6 4 2

British Library Cataloguing-in-Publication Data:
A catalogue record for this book is available from the British Library.

Commissioned by Liz Dean
Designed by Claire Graham
Edited by Ian Kearey and Christine Lee

Reproduction by Classic Scan Pte Ltd, Singapore
Printed by Leo Paper Products, China.

CONTENTS

INTRODUCTION

•

Associated with luck, fertility, love and prosperity, the power of the Moon can be felt throughout our lives.

INTRODUCTION

•

WHAT MOON SIGNS CAN DO FOR YOU

MOST PEOPLE KNOW their Sun sign, which is also called your sign of the zodiac or star sign. The Earth has a regular annual orbit around the Sun. Therefore, from an astrologer's point of view, the Sun moves through the signs of Capricorn and Aquarius in January, Aquarius and Pisces in February, and so on throughout the year. Up to now, there has been no instant way of knowing the position of the Moon on the day of your birth. *Moon Signs* changes all that by making it easy to discover the sign that the Moon occupied on the date you were born. Armed with this information, your inner nature will be revealed, and you will also discover your dreams, desires, emotional requirements, vulnerabilities, hidden failings and faults. Once you have looked into your own secret nature, you can then start to uncover the secret and hidden sides of your lovers, friends, colleagues and children. You can also use this book to look at the childhood influences that shaped you, and the less obvious characteristics that have lead you into the kind of career and relationships which have become part of your life.

THE RISING SIGN

Moon Signs also shows you how to find your rising sign. In simple terms, the Earth makes one complete revolution on its axis every 24 hours, and it is this that makes the Sun appear to rise, reach its apex, fall and set. We can't fail to be aware of the Sun's movement and we often know which part of our home or workplace the Sun shines on at various times of the day. However, we are less aware of the constellations of stars that also appear to move around the Earth in exactly the same way. This means that during the course of every 24-hour period, each sign of the zodiac travels around the Earth. Therefore, your time, date and place of birth will determine exactly which sign was rising over it when you were born.

Moon Signs will show you exactly how to work this out in a few minutes. The Rising Sign wheel in the pocket is less accurate than a professional astrologer's computer software, but you can still find your rising sign. However, any wheel such as this will be slightly imprecise, so if you feel that the rising sign indicated for you doesn't fit your nature, read about the one that precedes and follows it, and you will soon spot your own rising sign.

Your rising sign is often projected outwardly more clearly than even your Sun sign, so it is your rising sign that others will pick up. People who share the same rising sign usually have an instant rapport and get on very well in everyday situations. However, when it comes to the deeper experiences of living and loving in a close relationship, it is a combination of your rising sign, your Sun sign and that hidden emotional side of your nature, as shown by your Moon sign, that counts.

> *"'What do you think of it, Moon,*
> *As you go?*
> *Is life much or no?"*
> *"O, I think of it, often think of it*
> *As a show*
> *God ought surely to shut up soon*
> *As I go."'*
>
> Thomas Hardy, *To the Moon*

CREATING A MOON HOROSCOPE

By learning how to progress your natal Sun and Moon, you can quickly discover how the present moment is affecting you. A fascinating experiment is to look back to a particularly eventful year in your life and see exactly how the Moon was operating within your chart at that time. You might like to look at the present time or perhaps a year or two into the future to see what kind of atmosphere will be surrounding you, and what issues will be paramount in your life at that point in time. All this is easy to do with *Moon Signs*.

You can also work out the day-to-day transits of the Sun and Moon to get a daily horoscope – similar to those in newspapers, but as it refers to the Moon against your own horoscope, passing through the signs and houses, it will be far more accurate. If you are planning a special event or a particular activity, *Moon Signs* will help *you* to choose the right date.

So prepare to find out all about your hidden self and the secret yearnings that may be hidden deep inside your loved ones, check out your friends – and dare we say it – your enemies too!

LUNAR ASSOCIATIONS

•

The first thing that any astrologer learns is that the Moon is associated with emotions, motherhood, the family and domestic life.

FEMININE MOON, MASCULINE SUN

The ancient astrologer priests of Babylon and Sumeria saw the Sun as a *masculine* force of determination, success and worldly achievement. The *feminine* Moon was considered to rule womankind. In the old days (with rare exceptions) to be a woman meant that once adolescence was reached, motherhood beckoned. Mothers were considered to be far more important to the care and development of young children than fathers. The paternal role came along later, when boys were taught to ride, hunt and assume the masculine role of running the tribal group. Girls learned the crafts of womanhood from the older females who surrounded them.

Women were allowed to be emotional, whereas men had to be strong and fearless. This division was necessary for the group to survive, so feelings and emotions became linked to the feminine Moon. This bipolar energy is similar to the Chinese concept of yin and yang.

Astrologers learn that the Sun acts while the Moon reacts. Once again, these ideas go back to an age where the differences in the roles of men and women were far more marked, as indeed they still are in many parts of the world. Men were encouraged to make choices and to take decisions, while women had to make the best of whatever circumstances they found themselves in.

'The innocent moon, which nothing does but shine Moves all the labouring surges of the world.'

Francis Thompson, *Sister Songs*

MOON MYTHOLOGY

In Roman mythology the Moon was known as Diana, goddess of the chase, who was also the Greek Artemis, twin sister of the solar god Apollo. Artemis represented instincts as opposed to her brother's more rational approach. However, this free-spirited, wild-maiden goddess had more than one side to her complex

'A New Moon falling on a Saturday or a Sunday was thought to foretell a month of bad luck and worse weather.'

character. As the many-breasted Artemis, she was the archetypal mother-goddess nurturing the world, while at the same time she was Hecate, goddess of the Underworld, worshipped by witches at crossroads in the dead of night.

These three aspects represent the triple goddess: the maiden, the mother and the crone, probably the most ancient deity to be worshipped by mankind. Her influence has stretched from the earliest days of our prehistory through every human civilization. In Egypt the lunar nurturing role was taken by Isis, in Babylon by Ishtar, while in Northern Europe she was known by a host of names, including Eostra, the ancient Anglo-Saxon goddess of fertility after whom the festival of Easter is named. The ancient Celts of Britain and Ireland never forgot the triple nature of their deity and called her Brid, Ceridwen and Morrigan. Morrigan went on to become Morgan le Fay in Arthurian tradition, while Brid was Christianized as St Brigid who, among other things, became at different times the patron saint of nuns, dairy workers, cows, midwives, babies, fugitives, sailors, Ireland, Wales, Australia and New Zealand. Many of these are still governed by the Moon in astrology today.

Cows, dairies, milkmaids, milk-churns, butter, cheese and everything else that has to do with milk was considered to be feminine and therefore lunar. The men were generally out working in the forests and farms, and it was most often the women who milked the cows and made butter and cheese.

As time progressed and iceboxes and refrigerators were invented, these too became associated in updated astrological thinking with the influences of the Moon. Following on from this, the kitchen, the stove and everything concerning food became attached to the Moon. The women who cooked and looked after the home were therefore especially associated with the lunar principle. The kitchen was at the centre of the woman's realm and took on an archetypal significance. No matter how far this may be from the actual truth, there is still a strong appeal in this

idyllic folk memory of a kitchen filled with the aroma of baking bread, clean linen being run through a mangle, and the love and warmth of a good family home. This provided an emotional ideal that was firmly placed under the rulership of the maternal Moon.

THE MOON AND THE SEA

The Moon was associated with the sea because of the ancient belief that when it was not visible in the sky, it disappeared somewhere under the sea. Sailors have always known that the movement of the Moon affects the tides, so the Moon became associated with sailing and especially with sailors. Fishing also originally came under the influence of the Moon. Sailors could always sew, as they needed to mend sails and nets and make or mend their own clothes when at sea; therefore handiness with a needle also fell under the realm of the Moon.

Modern astrologers now link travel to planets such as Mercury and Jupiter, but in the old days, travel (especially travel across water) was considered to be a lunar event. To the ancients, restlessness and a footloose nature became a lunar trait. The restless motion of the Moon, with its tendency to disappear into the sea once a month, allied to its emotional female nature, suggested that moodiness, changeability and complex behaviour were lunar characteristics. This led to the idea that a person who was irrational was a luna-tic. There are plenty of anecdotal accounts of unstable people who behave badly at the time of the Full Moon (this phenomenon seems to be borne out by the statistician Michel Gauquelin's mammoth studies of astrological effects). Even in these aggressively scientific times, there is a belief that hospitals and police stations are busier at the time of the Full Moon.*

THE MOON AND THE TIDES

The most noticeable effect the Moon has on the Earth is the phenomenon of the tides. With majestic regularity the Moon causes the ebb and flow of the waters of our planet, and since

* *The Truth about Astrology*, Michel Gauquelin, Hutchinson, 1983

ASTRONOMICAL INFLUENCES

•

The motion of the Moon is connected with those of the Sun and the Earth. This is so complicated that the same position is never, ever repeated, and yet all three perform a celestial dance of such elegant perfection that their movements are predictable.

Currently, it is thought that some large impacts long in the past caused pieces of the Earth to break off. These molten rocks gathered in orbit and eventually joined together to form our Moon. Many further asteroid impacts over a period of 500 million years created the Moon's familiar pitted surface.

The Moon does not orbit the centre of the Earth. Both Earth and Moon revolve around a common centre of gravity called the barycentre, which lies 1,610 km (1,000 miles) below the Earth's surface, approximately 4,825 km (3,000 miles) out from the core.

The mass of the Earth is 81 times that of the Moon, which circles approximately 384,320 km (238,857 miles) at a speed of 1 km (0.63 miles) per second.

Both the Earth and the Moon have had quite a battering over the course of their long histories. A glance at the pitted, cratered surface of the Moon proves that it has been hit by many asteroids since its formation. The Earth too has been on the receiving end of numerous impacts, but our weather systems have eroded the scars.

The Moon's craters range in size from tiny pits to huge areas with walled plains and central peaks. The crater Clavius is more than 225 km (140 miles) across and bears witness to a devastating impact long ago.

The recent discovery of water in the form of ice on the Moon makes the prospect of colonization more likely in the foreseeable future. Perhaps astrologers will soon have to work out a way of creating a horoscope from the viewpoint of the Moon.

our bodies are over 90 per cent water, the Moon also causes the ebb and flow of our moods and emotions.

The link between the lunar cycle and the tides was first noticed (as far as anyone can establish the fact) by the ancient Chinese. However, we in the West were slower to catch on to this fact because the sages of Greece and Rome hardly noticed any changes in the generally calm Mediterranean sea. It is claimed that the Romans only found out about the turbulence of the oceans when they colonized Britain and were exposed to the wild Atlantic.

The explanation of the rhythmic motion of the water is a simple one. The gravitational pull of the Moon, our closest astral neighbour, is so strong that it draws the Earth's water towards it. This causes the seas to lift in the direction of the Moon. This of course will cause a high tide in that area of the Earth. Equally, on the side of the Earth that points away from our lunar partner the tide will be low.

The highest tides occur at the New Moon when Earth, Moon and Sun are in alignment. The reason for this is that the Sun's massive gravitational pull is added to that of the Moon at this time. These are often called spring tides. The lowest tides will occur one week after the New and Full Moons when the Sun is at 90 degrees to the Earth, making the gravitational pulls of the Moon and the Sun almost cancel each other out. These minimal movements of water are usually referred to as neap tides.

It is a sobering thought to consider that even though the phenomenon of tides is most obvious in the world's oceans, the Moon has a tidal effect on any body of liquid, including a cup of tea or coffee. So ask yourself, what effect does our lunar companion have on our body fluids, the blood that courses through our veins or the liquid that surrounds our brains?

*'The sun to me is dark
And silent as the moon,
When she deserts the night
Hid in her vacant,
interlunar cave.'*

John Milton, *Samson Agonistes*

LOOKING BACKWARDS

Another idea associated with the Moon is the desire to look backwards. People who are interested in history often have a strongly placed Moon in their chart, and the Moon is often found in the first, fourth, seventh or tenth house of their horoscope. In some cases this interest in past times leads them to collect

'It is a good idea to turn over the change in your pocket when a New Moon is seen, to ensure prosperity through the coming month.'

antiques, old coins or other items of historical significance, while in others it leads to patriotism (occasionally xenophobia), or simply an interest in the history of their country.

THE MOON AND PUBLIC LIFE

With all the emphasis on the inner life of the emotions and the private life of the home, it is difficult to see why the Moon is also associated with the public – or more specifically, dealing with the public. The idea here is that the lunar part of a horoscope reflects your affinity with other people and their needs. For example, people who work in the public service often have a strong Moon affecting their charts, while those whose principal interests are simply to serve themselves have a stronger solar influence.

So, now that you have looked at the astrological influence of the Moon in detail, you can learn how to find and use these fascinating astrological features with the help of *Moon Signs*.

UNDERSTANDING YOUR MOON SIGN

•

Your Moon sign reveals your inner nature – your dreams, desires and 'emotional intelligence'.

FINDING YOUR MOON SIGN

ARIES

TAURUS

GEMINI

CANCER

LEO

VIRGO

LIBRA

SCORPIO

SAGITTARIUS

CAPRICORN

AQUARIUS

PISCES

FIND THE YEAR OF YOUR BIRTH in the year column of the chart on page 19 and then read across to the appropriate month column. Write down the star sign listed. Then look for the day of your birth on the table below and note the number underneath. Now go to the column of zodiac signs immediately on the left and simply count that number on from the star sign you found in the month column of the chart. This is your Moon sign. For example, if you were born on 17 January 1972, find 1972 in the year column of the chart on page 19, then move across to January in the month column, and you will find the sign of Cancer. Then look up 17 in the table below, the result being the number 7. Count 7 on from Cancer (in the column, left) to reveal your Moon sign of Aquarius.

EXACT DAY OF BIRTH

1	2	3	4	5	6	7	8
0	1	1	1	2	2	3	3
9	10	11	12	13	14	15	16
4	4	5	5	5	6	6	7
17	18	19	20	21	22	23	24
7	8	8	9	9	10	10	10
25	26	27	28	29	30	31	
11	11	12	12	1	1	2	

YEAR					MONTH											
					JAN	FEB	MAR	APR	MAY	JUN	JUL	AUG	SEP	OCT	NOV	DEC
1920	1939	1958	1977	1996	Tau	Can	Can	Vir	Lib	Sag	Cap	Aqu	Ari	Tau	Can	Leo
1921	1940	1959	1978	1997	Lib	Sco	Sag	Cap	Aqu	Ari	Tau	Can	Leo	Vir	Sco	Sag
1922	1941	1960	1979	1998	Aqu	Ari	Ari	Gem	Can	Leo	Vir	Sco	Cap	Aqu	Ari	Tau
1923	1942	1961	1980	1999	Gem	Leo	Leo	Lib	Sco	Cap	Aqu	Ari	Tau	Gem	Leo	Vir
1924	1943	1962	1981	2000	Sco	Sag	Cap	Aqu	Ari	Tau	Gem	Leo	Lib	Sco	Sag	Cap
1925	1944	1963	1982	2001	Pis	Tau	Tau	Can	Leo	Lib	Sco	Sag	Aqu	Pis	Tau	Gem
1926	1945	1964	1983	2002	Leo	Vir	Lib	Sco	Sag	Aqu	Pis	Tau	Can	Leo	Vir	Lib
1927	1946	1965	1984	2003	Sag	Cap	Aqu	Pis	Tau	Gem	Leo	Vir	Sco	Sag	Aqu	Pis
1928	1947	1966	1985	2004	Ari	Gem	Gem	Leo	Vir	Sco	Sag	Aqu	Pis	Ari	Gem	Can
1929	1948	1967	1986	2005	Vir	Sco	Sco	Cap	Aqu	Pis	Tau	Gem	Leo	Vir	Lib	Sag
1930	1949	1968	1987	2006	Cap	Pis	Pis	Tau	Gem	Leo	Vir	Sco	Sag	Cap	Pis	Ari
1931	1950	1969	1988	2007	Tau	Can	Can	Vir	Lib	Sag	Cap	Pis	Ari	Gem	Can	Leo
1932	1951	1970	1989	2008	Lib	Sag	Sag	Aqu	Pis	Tau	Gem	Can	Vir	Lib	Sag	Cap
1933	1952	1971	1990	2009	Pis	Ari	Tau	Gem	Can	Vir	Lib	Sag	Cap	Aqu	Ari	Tau
1934	1953	1972	1991	2010	Can	Vir	Vir	Lib	Sag	Cap	Pis	Ari	Gem	Can	Vir	Lib
1935	1954	1973	1992		Sco	Cap	Cap	Pis	Ari	Gem	Can	Vir	Sco	Sag	Cap	Aqu
1936	1955	1974	1993		Ari	Tau	Gem	Leo	Vir	Lib	Sco	Cap	Pis	Ari	Tau	Can
1937	1956	1975	1994		Leo	Lib	Lib	Sag	Cap	Pis	Ari	Tau	Can	Leo	Lib	Sco
1938	1957	1976	1995		Cap	Aqu	Pis	Ari	Tau	Can	Leo	Lib	Sco	Cap	Aqu	Ari

MOON IN ARIES

YOU ARE A quick thinker, talker and large-scale planner, but you may need help with specific details. Lunar Ariens are often starters rather than runners, so you may be happier as an executive rather than as an ordinary worker. You may be a tough go-getter, but your confidence can evaporate quickly and you need the support and admiration of others.

Women with this Moon placement may value a career highly. You can be enthusiastic, headstrong and freedom-loving, unable to accept restrictions or unnecessary discipline. Your love life may be stormy, either because you are changeable and easily bored or because you are unwilling to compromise. However, you are probably honest and don't try to manipulate others.

Moon in Aries people can be deft and dextrous, so your excellent co-ordination could make you successful at many sports.

The Moon is a 'watery' planet, and when it is in a fire sign emotions can be expressed quickly and easily. Moon Ariens can therefore display a hot temper, although you usually cool down quickly and rarely sulk. It may be hard to get you to listen to others, as you tend to see everything from your own point of view, concentrating on your own emotional needs rather than those of others.

One problem that seems to afflict those with the Moon in Aries is that of having a domineering or difficult parent, and the years from adolescence to independence are often characterized by shouting matches.

MOON IN TAURUS

THIS IS SUPPOSED to be the most stable and comfortable placement for the Moon, but you may only be really content when your life is in perfect working order. Although you may be able to deal with practical problems very efficiently, when emotional problems come along you can fall apart dramatically. Many Moon in Taurus people have a pleasant manner and are sociable, reliable and honest, needing a happy family life, a comfortable home and a good job. You would make a good parent and get on well with your family. You rarely lose contact with your children even when they become adults.

Lunar Taureans who are loving, affectionate and romantic can also be highly sexed. You may enter relationships with the best of intentions and only leave when there is no other recourse. You might not have many close friends, and if so, you might not always be generous with time or money to those outside your own circle. If possessive, jealous and stubborn, you need stability and will try hard to uphold the status quo. You may have a formidable temper and can become destructive when you feel threatened.

You can be tough but fair in business, and can have good luck financially, whether making money for yourself or working in an area where you handle large contracts worth a lot of money on behalf of others.

Most Moon in Taurus subjects love music, gardening, anything to do with nature and the outdoors, and travelling.

MOON IN GEMINI

YOU PROBABLY HAVE an active mind which may be academic, creative, imaginative or logical, depending upon other features in your birthchart. You may be dextrous and versatile and able to cope with most tasks around the home. You can work well under supervision, as long as you respect your superiors. Lunar Geminis who need to feel free may avoid getting involved in personal relationships altogether, but if you do marry you will probably need a practical but easy-going partner. You may enjoy mental pursuits such as reading books, playing games or using computers, or gentle sports such as snooker and golf.

Lunar Geminis often work in large organizations that provide a service to the public, such as banking or the travel trade, journalism or teaching, and you are likely to have many friends and acquaintances whom you met through your work. Lunar Geminis can be excellent teachers and make good parents, but women need the stimulation of a job outside the home. Both sexes are good home-makers, but may find it hard to relax as they are prone to worrying.

You may become the planner and thinker for your family and they may depend upon your fine logical mind.

MOON IN CANCER

AS THE MOON is the ruler of the sign of Cancer, it is at its most comfortable in this sign and its intrinsic characteristics are heightened. Lunar Cancerians are often emotional, sensitive and moody. You can be imaginative and creative, and appreciate music and the arts. Being naturally intuitive, you can be drawn to psychic or mystical matters, but can be equally at home in the world of business and finance.

You can be emotionally demanding, requiring endless love and affection, often making your loved ones feel guilty for failing to meet your emotional demands. Sometimes you may even use emotional blackmail to get your own way. Not all lunar Cancerians are this difficult, however, and you can be very supportive when in a happy relationship.

Lunar Cancerians tend to make good family members and excellent parents, and they are often drawn into teaching or take on a training role in their careers. Alternatively, they may work in one of the caring professions. You may be unwelcoming or suspicious of strangers, or simply shy and nervous. You can be shrewd in business matters which, coupled with your intuition and capacity for hard work, helps to make you very successful. You may not like taking chances and need financial and emotional security, planning well for your old age.

Your ideal holiday would be one where you can relax by the sea and take boat trips.

MOON IN LEO

 MOON IN LEO subjects tend to have a sunny disposition and be friendly, welcoming and approachable. Rarely hostile or suspicious, you can be genuinely confident or simply able to put on a display of confidence when it is needed.

Loyal, loving and idealistic people rarely leave a relationship unless it becomes absolutely necessary. If you find yourself alone, you may attach yourself to a new family or form one again fairly quickly. You are likely to be happiest in both personal and business relationships where partners and colleagues understand and admire you.

Lunar Leos can put themselves, their partners or their children on a pedestal, expecting more than is possible from them. You can be excellent organizers who enjoy an orderly life, but you also have a tendency to be bossy and arrogant, while at other times being helpless – especially when ill. You take on responsibility well and make a good leader.

There are also likely to be times when you simply switch off and go through a period of relaxation and laziness. This is simply because you need to rest to stay healthy. You may feel that you are 'special' in some way, have a lot of style, and actually have some great talent or ability.

You often fuss and worry about your appearance, especially your hair, which may be long and full like a lion's mane.

MOON IN VIRGO

YOU MAY BE keenly intellectual, discriminating and capable of dealing with details. You can work hard at a project that interests you, but can also switch right off and become surprisingly lazy. The most important thing to bear in mind is that you can be emotionally contained. You might keep your emotions on such a tight leash that you never give yourself permission to express your real needs and feelings. If you don't find some form of emotional release, perhaps through group counselling, you could make yourself ill. Lunar Virgos can be embarrassed by displays of emotion by other people, but you can put on a wonderful display of tears and temper yourself when in the mood to do so. You can also express negative emotions through being far too critical towards your loved ones.

Moon in Virgo folk are often interested in matters of health, hygiene, fitness, diet and alternative therapies. This might have been thrust upon you through some kind of long-term health problem, or simply derives from a life-long interest. Lunar Virgoans can be excellent cooks and home-makers, and may hate to live in a dirty or messy environment. If you are an animal lover, you probably have a pet of some kind around the house.

You work hard to provide the necessities of life for yourself and your family, but you may be too nervous, shy and sensitive to aim for a top job. In this case your ideal job would be one where you are appreciated by those above you and are also useful to the world in general. If you are shrewd and clever, and can make and keep money, you can also be a little stingy. Many lunar Virgoans work in the health field or in anything to do with books and information technology.

MOON IN LIBRA

YOU CAN BE charming, optimistic, outgoing and sociable. You may be a skilled and tactful diplomat who is popular at work and in all kinds of social settings. Lunar Librans can appear weak or soft, but you can also be ambitious, hardworking and determined, especially when you have a goal in sight. Those lunar Librans who don't like being alone for too long seek out company and need partnerships in business and personal life. You often have many friends and acquaintances. In earlier times, these people often married young, but nowadays they may try living with a series of partners until they find the right person to spend their lives with. You can be faithful when in a relationship, but may also be extremely flirtatious.

You can be fussy about decor and colour schemes, and could make an excellent architect, interior designer or film-set or software designer. Your diplomatic skills could take you into agency work, marketing or any area that involves negotiating, where you can prove to be a surprisingly tough negotiator. Although happy and cheerful most of the time, you can be unpleasant, sarcastic and downright nasty when someone really upsets you. You may be arrogant, and can argue the hind leg off a donkey, never backing down from a fight. For all your fussiness, you can be untidy, especially when busy working. Many lunar Librans are musical or artistic.

You may spend your life seeking perfection either in the form of an ideal home or a perfect lover.

MOON IN SCORPIO

WHENEVER THE MOON is in a water sign the emotions are intense, and in Scorpio they can be either well-hidden or very close to the surface. If you are the inward-looking type, you will take your feelings seriously; if you are let down in love, you can drive your friends and family crazy by continually harping on about your disappointment. Conversely, you might never mention your troubles but allow them to fester.

Lunar Scorpios can be moody, secretive and hard to understand. While you never forget a hurt, you can also be intensely loyal and loving to those who are good to you, and won't readily forget favours or obligations. You hate to owe money, and do not care for those who borrow from you and then fail to pay you back.

Lunar Scorpios may do best when allied to a cheerful, capable and emotionally stable partner, but your vulnerability can lead you to select a sensitive or even chaotic mate. Although stubborn and inclined to stick with your choices, you can be driven to leave a relationship. However, many lunar Scorpios do learn from their mistakes and go on to make better choices in the future. Sex can be used (or withdrawn) as a weapon. Magnetic, determined and sometimes manipulative, you can be extremely fascinating. Your intense nature can be relieved by a terrific sense of humour, a wonderful sense of justice and a fondness for the underdog in any situation. Lunar Scorpios can be strangely sympathetic, and they are often deeply loving.

MOON IN SAGITTARIUS

A DISPROPORTIONATE NUMBER of people with the Moon in Sagittarius work in the psychic field, and many are excellent astrologers, dowsers, palmists and just about anything else with an intuitive slant. It seems that the Sagittarian urge to explore takes an inward turn when the Moon is in this sign, leading you to seek enlightenment at a deep inner level. Superficially, lunar Sagittarians can be optimistic, outgoing and friendly. You may travel a great deal, or may have strong connections with people from different cultures. Some lunar Sagittarians feel the need to contact as many people as they can during their lifetime, so this may lead you to choose jobs in such areas as broadcasting, teaching or the travel trade – astrology is a great way of meeting people, of course.

Lunar Sagittarians who need personal freedom can find marriage or a permanent commitment too confining, but you can sustain friendships for years. You may be better at friendship than marriage, and if so, you probably manage to maintain friendly relationships with ex-partners and their extended families throughout your life. You are usually fond of animals, especially dogs and horses, and probably have a pet.

You may find it hard to stick to a job, but if you can find one that is interesting and varied enough for your tastes, you will stay with it. You can be surprisingly ambitious and competitive, which may lead you into a sporting or competition-based lifestyle.

MOON IN CAPRICORN

LUNAR CAPRICORNS MAY be extremely shy and uncertain when it comes to making friends or enjoying any kind of social life. If you find someone to love and care for, you can overcome this, gain courage and confidence and open up to others later on. You may choose an older partner who has the maturity you need, and possibly one who will also mother or father you. Lunar Capricorns may do well in their career, taking work a little too seriously at times, but nevertheless often enjoying the success and financial rewards that it brings. Alternatively, you might never really get a proper career off the ground, preferring to stay in a menial job where there is no chance of failure. Fear and lack of confidence appear to be the main problems, but if they can be overcome, success is assured. In some cases, power and status can be viewed as a compensation for emotional emptiness.

You probably have a good head for business, but you can spoil your chances of real success by being short-sighted. If you do well in business, then often you will become emotionally involved in your job and your life may lack balance as a result.

You may be so attached to a parent that you never really let go of them; at best, including your parent or parents in your own marital and family life. At worst, you may not leave the parental home at all, remaining single for much, if not all, of your life.

MOON IN AQUARIUS

 MANY LUNAR AQUARIANS need independence in their marriages and careers – you cannot live under someone else's thumb or be dictated to by others. If you have to face a particularly difficult situation, you may prefer to do this on your own and without an audience; if you have to go into hospital, you won't allow anyone to visit until you look presentable again.

You can be extremely imaginative, innovative and creative. You may have plenty of good ideas to pass on to others, and there is nothing you like better than to be asked for your advice. Under stress, you can become gossipy, aloof or sarcastic, and even unpredictable. You can be broadminded, always up-to-date and keen to live life to the full.

Lunar Aquarians can be quite tough to live with, due to your extreme independence and self-contained attitude. You may be obstinate, awkward, argumentative and determined, and you are very keen on having your own way. You need a partner you can respect and rely upon, and in this case the partner will need to be as strong and independent as you are. You are usually friendly and are never at a loss for company when you fancy it; kind, loyal and steadfast, you are often quick to help an underdog or adopt a lame duck.

You value education and will do all you can to ensure that your children have as good an education as possible. Travel appeals to you, as you enjoy seeing new things and meeting a variety of people.

MOON IN PISCES

 THIS PLACEMENT CAN bring about an unusual lifestyle. Those lunar Pisceans who are mystical, psychic and extremely sensitive can be moody and prone to terrible depression from time to time. This Moon placement suggests vulnerability and shyness, but this may often be covered up well in later life. The continual presence of other people can upset you and disturb the delicate balance of your psyche or aura. You may act as a psychic sponge, picking up the moods and vibrations of those you come into contact with, so a little time alone will be needed in order to clear the aura of unwanted vibrations.

In some cases, low self-esteem and apathy can prevent you from achieving anything, but if you have a strong, supportive, practical, sensible and loving partner, you can blossom.

If loved and cared for, you offer love, devotion and faithfulness on a level that few others can provide. Sympathetic and caring, romantic and loving, you may be too soft and delicate to cope with the rough-and-tumble of daily life. However, you also have a tensile inner strength and a feeling of psychic protection that comes to your aid in times of crisis. You may have a magical gift for helping those who are troubled. Timid, retiring and possibly suffering from poor health, you may achieve more, show more courage and cope with more than all the other Moon signs put together — as long as you keep away from the twin demons of drink and drugs!

THE MOON AND CHILDHOOD

THE MOON IN ARIES CHILD

Children with the Moon in the sign of Aries, the Ram, are generally independent-natured. Perhaps they have been forced into standing on their own two feet and taking responsibility for themselves from an early age. Even if circumstances do not actually force this course of action, there will still be an inclination to become the captain of their own destinies when very young. The mother may be perceived as being strong, capable and rather forceful. These are qualities that a lunar Aries will emulate in later life.

THE MOON IN TAURUS CHILD

The charm of lunar Taurean children is evident. They have a way with adults which generally allows them to get their own way even if they have to be patient and wait a while for things to fall into place. Patience, though, is something that lunar Taureans have no trouble acquiring. There is also a very mature side to them, ensuring that communicating with adults is much easier for them than for other children.

Their responsible attitudes, charming manner and stable character are traits they will carry with them into adulthood.

THE MOON IN GEMINI CHILD

As long as there is plenty to capture the lively curiosity of the lunar Geminian child, there will be few problems in dealing with this youngster. The only worry is that they have a low boredom threshold and a very active mind, so keeping them mentally occupied constantly could become a nightmare. Fortunately, parents need not put too much effort into keeping their child's attention occupied because lunar Geminis are quite capable of amusing themselves. This is all well and good, but keep your eyes peeled for mischief.

THE MOON IN CANCER CHILD

From the very beginning, the lunar Cancerian will be firmly focused on home, family, heritage and most particularly their relationship with their mothers and older women of their clan. The lunar Cancerian child has very strong instincts and will solve most problems by a tendency to leap suddenly to a conclusion, even if logic doesn't back it up. The amazing thing is that they are likely to be right! The protective and nurturing instincts of this most lunar of signs cannot be underestimated. From an early age they will be busy looking after other children and even fussing over adults.

*'The Moon is associated with
the sign of Cancer.'*

THE MOON IN LEO CHILD

Lunar lions were born for the stage, or at least for a lifetime spent in the spotlight, so they can be quite a handful when they aren't receiving the attention that they absolutely know is their divine right! Little lunar Leos seem to inherit their flamboyance from their mothers or other strong female influences and their sense of authority from their fathers. Even when small, they can put an adult in his place and can be prone to lecturing their elders. Both parents will tend to be very ambitious for their child.

THE MOON IN VIRGO CHILD

The self-discipline of the lunar Virgo has its origins in childhood. Home life may have been somewhat strict, or at least it may have seemed that way to a highly sensitive lunar Virgo child. Lunar Virgo children may be shy or withdrawn in some way and will need a lot of encouragement to express themselves. It is also important for them to have a private corner of their own in which they can play out complex fantasy games without the interference of more boisterous children.

The lunar Virgo child may be rather quiet, but that mind is going at full pelt and those little eyes and ears will miss nothing.

THE MOON IN LIBRA CHILD

Charm, creativity and artistic flair are evident from an early age in children with the Moon in the balanced sign of Libra. Beauty and harmony are very important to these sensitive souls and it would be too easy for them to become withdrawn in the company of rougher, more boisterous children. Teasing can be a particular problem if adults do not notice and let the situation go unchecked. Often, the mother is over-indulgent of the lunar Libran child and consequently the child grows up getting his or her own way in most things.

THE MOON IN SCORPIO CHILD

Many of the lunar Scorpio traits come from childhood influences, especially from a strong mother. In fact, the lunar Scorpio tendency to admire strong, capable women often stems from the image of the mother as someone who could cope with anything. This is what the Moon in Scorpio child wants for himself or herself. This child will be very determined and, taking the cue from older females in the family, be supportive and helpful to younger friends and siblings. However, if asked, they would say that all is well as long as they get exactly what they want.

THE MOON IN SAGITTARIUS CHILD

A child with the Moon in Sagittarius is often born into very different circumstances from those of his or her parents. Traditionally this placement often means that the parents have moved from one country to another or that their wealth is either vastly greater or less than when they were children. In extreme cases parents and child have different first languages and cultural backgrounds. This gives lunar Sagittarian children a sensitivity to differences and makes them non-judgemental, perceptive and even psychic. Certainly they will have a splendid imagination, be adventurous and yearn for distant travel.

'The moonstone protects against absorbing the emotions of others and prevents depression.'

THE MOON IN CAPRICORN CHILD

Children with the Moon in Capricorn often have a close affinity to, and tend to resemble, their fathers. At least that's the traditional view. Most often, though, they tend to take after the dominant parent, whether father or mother. Either way, their life lessons start early and they soon absorb the values of the older generation. This is a factor that will be with them throughout their lives. The concepts of hard work, attaining high standards and respect will be far more important than sentiment or overt displays of affection. The phrase 'an old head on young shoulders' fits a lunar Capricorn child perfectly.

> *'O! swear not by the moon,
> the inconstant moon,
> That monthly changes in
> her circled orb,
> Lest thy love prove likewise
> variable.'*
>
> William Shakespeare, *Romeo and Juliet*

THE MOON IN AQUARIUS CHILD

True to form, lunar Aquarians are unconventional from the start. It is quite likely that they come from a household that is unconventional in some way. There may be a marked age difference between their parents or they have a rather progressive attitude towards their children. Possibly the home is filled with electronic equipment, computers, DVD players and similar paraphernalia. How else could the child with the Moon in quick-thinking Aquarius have such a skill with complex devices of all kinds? Having said that, an eccentric start in life is not easily forgotten and the individualistic lunar Aquarian child will turn into an extremely individualistic adult.

THE MOON IN PISCES CHILD

A child with the Moon in the gentle sign of Pisces must be the most sensitive and impressionable in the whole of the zodiac. Such children are prone to psychic awareness from a very early age and this trait will probably continue throughout their lives. The mother and older female relatives will be the most potent influence in formative years and this emphasis on nurturing becomes even more important when one realizes that the little lunar Pisces tends not to have an easy time of it. Being so emotionally delicate, hurt is always close at hand, and even with the best will in the world, cannot really be avoided. At least the lunar Piscean will grow into a charitable and caring adult.

THE MOON AND YOUR CAREER

This section of the book is very different from every other astrology book that is around. This is because when you are looking, by the light of the Moon, at the type of job you might do, the picture becomes hard to see, rather like trying to find one's way around by moonlight. There are plenty of books that list jobs under the more familiar Sun sign types (Aries for soldiers and Scorpio for surgeons, for example), but this doesn't work when we look at it from a lunar point of view, because the Moon rules your inner urges and the way you secretly feel about your life.

MOON IN ARIES

Some of you prefer to work in a large organization where there is a definite career structure, but where you can wield a certain amount of authority. In this instance, you don't seem to have the kind of self-motivation that would enable you to become self-employed.

MOON IN TAURUS

Taurus rules work in the fields of beauty or harmony, but this is not what the lunar Taurean looks for. You may go where the money is, and if that happens to be in engineering, computing or banking, that is where we would expect to find you.

MOON IN GEMINI

You may want to work with the public in a helpful manner, so a job that incorporates sales work and also enables you to act as an advisor would suit you well. In this situation, the telephone is your close companion and you may prefer to deal with people by phone rather than face to face.

MOON IN CANCER

The caring professions may suit you, with teaching children at the top of the list. Anything to do with property or premises, such as selling or letting might suit you, as would any small business where you can deal directly with the public.

MOON IN LEO

Although the specific field that you choose to work in is unimportant, you may feel a great need for status and a high income. Like your Cancerian neighbour, you may be a shrewd property dealer, but in your case, the scale of your operations would be much bigger.

> *'So, we'll go no more a roving*
> *So late into the night,*
> *Though the heart be still*
> *as loving,*
> *And the moon be still as bright.'*
>
> Lord Byron,
> *So we'll go no more a roving*

MOON IN VIRGO

The caring professions are unlikely to ring the same bell for lunar Virgoans that they do for Sun in Virgo people. If words, ideas and figurework are much more your forte, any kind of publishing, editing, secretarial or record-keeping work would suit you. Many lunar Virgoans also work in the field of information technology.

MOON IN LIBRA

Negotiating and wheeler-dealing may suit you well, as you can usually get your way in these fields without upsetting people. High-status jobs are nice, but good money is even better, so a job in the financial or business world would suit you.

MOON IN SCORPIO

Your job must involve more than simply doing something for the money, so you may have the urge to help or care for less fortunate people. Healing and therapy work might suit your needs. You may have a deft touch with animals.

MOON IN SAGITTARIUS

Many astrologers have the Moon in Sagittarius, as do many spiritual people. Teaching and broadcasting are other possibilities. Breeding or training horses, or dealing with animals can suit lunar Sagittarians even more than it does Sun in Sagittarius types.

'The Queen of Night,
whose large command
Rules all the sea,
and half the land.'

Samuel Butler, *Hudibras*

MOON IN CAPRICORN

You may work in some field that keeps you close to home or in touch with your family, so carrying on the family business might suit you. In this case, you may not make much money, but you will probably enjoy keeping busy and being useful to the public and to your family alike.

MOON IN AQUARIUS

Independence and originality are often the name of the game here. Design work, or any creative task where you can extract ideas from inside yourself and also from others and develop them into something useful or attractive, can work for you.

MOON IN PISCES

You may feel you instinctively know what the public needs, so you might seek to serve humanity in some way. Many lunar Pisceans work in the caring or teaching professions, and many more work as clairvoyants, healers, therapists, social workers and astrologers.

'The Chinese believe the Moon is the home of a hare who brews a potion of immortality. If you look at the Full Moon with your head to the right, an image of the lunar hare can be seen.'

YOUR MOON SIGN CHARACTERISTICS

Here is a selection of keywords to help you to remember the influence of the Moon in each of the signs of the zodiac. These keywords are equally valid for natal and predictive astrology. If you find that you exhibit some of the negative characteristics, this could be because you need to express more of the positive traits in your life.

THE MOON IN ARIES

POSITIVE TRAITS	NEGATIVE TRAITS
Spontaneous	Impetuous
Direct	Rude
Energetic	Frenzied
Open	Tactless
Assertive	Pushy
Original	Reckless

THE MOON IN TAURUS

POSITIVE TRAITS	NEGATIVE TRAITS
Consistent	Habit-ruled
Patient	Slow-reacting
Affectionate	Demanding
Sensuous	Lustful
Practical	Unimaginative
Determined	Narrow-minded

THE MOON IN GEMINI

POSITIVE TRAITS	NEGATIVE TRAITS
Light-hearted	Superficial
Witty	Chatterbox
Fast-moving	Restless
Versatile	Shallow
Conversational	Gossipy
Charming	Insincere

THE MOON IN CANCER

POSITIVE TRAITS	NEGATIVE TRAITS
Protective	Possessive
Sympathetic	Touchy
Dependable	One-sided
Introspective	Withdrawn
Emotional	Needy
Sensitive	Moody

THE MOON IN LEO

POSITIVE TRAITS	NEGATIVE TRAITS
Impressive	Demanding
Noble	Snobbish
Dramatic	Overbearing
Proud	Conceited
Dignified	Vain
Confident	Arrogant

THE MOON IN VIRGO

POSITIVE TRAITS	NEGATIVE TRAITS
Analytical	Pedantic
Conscientious	Anxiety-prone
Shrewd	Cold
Discriminating	Prejudiced
Neat	Neurotic
Respectable	Prudish

THE MOON IN LIBRA

POSITIVE TRAITS	NEGATIVE TRAITS
Romantic	Silly
Graceful	Superficial
Refined	Shallow
Friendly	Flirtatious
Relaxed	Lazy
Reasonable	Indecisive

THE MOON IN SCORPIO

POSITIVE TRAITS	NEGATIVE TRAITS
Intuitive	Suspicious
Passionate	Jealous
Independent	Lonely
Complex	Manipulative
Determined	Obsessive
Shrewd	Underhand

THE MOON IN SAGITTARIUS

POSITIVE TRAITS	NEGATIVE TRAITS
Philosophical	Unrealistic
Fun-loving	Irresponsible
Wise	Pompous
Generous	Foolish
Outspoken	Tactless
Trusting	Naive

THE MOON IN CAPRICORN

POSITIVE TRAITS	NEGATIVE TRAITS
Self-controlled	Repressed
Modest	Self-doubting
Cautious	Distrustful
Hardworking	Wage slave
Prudent	Boring
Ambitious	Ruthless

THE MOON IN AQUARIUS

POSITIVE TRAITS	NEGATIVE TRAITS
Broad-minded	Indiscriminate
Reforming	Rebellious
Cool	Cold
Progressive	Unpredictable
Original	Eccentric
Unbiased	Impersonal

THE MOON IN PISCES

POSITIVE TRAITS	NEGATIVE TRAITS
Imaginative	Escapist
Mystical	Deceptive
Empathic	Impressionable
Gentle	Weak
Caring	Martyr
Compassionate	Hypersensitive

THE MOON AND YOUR RELATIONSHIPS

You can tell a lot about your compatibility with a lover or friend by looking at your Moon sign and their Moon sign. Comparing the two signs will reveal how their inner personality will co-exist with your more emotional needs.

IF YOUR MOON IS IN ARIES

and your partner has their Moon in...

ARIES – There may be a lack of compromise but your independent natures are basically in harmony.

TAURUS – You may become irritated by your lover's stubbornness and desire for a comfortable stable life when you crave adventure.

GEMINI – Differences of opinion are inevitable, but you'll have enough in common to make this link-up work.

CANCER – Too much fussing from a lunar Cancerian will leave you cold, yet you must admit that there are times when you want to be coddled.

LEO – This is a sexual pairing with enough excitement to suit you both, though tempers are likely to flare up now and again.

VIRGO – This is likely to be a difficult combination with a lack of common ground in basic attitudes to life, love and sex.

LIBRA – It shouldn't work, but somehow it does. The charm of the lunar Libran could calm you down and make you happy.

SCORPIO – You have a little too much in common here. Everything that irritates will actually be too close to you for comfort. Jealousy and negative passions are likely.

SAGITTARIUS – There is never a dull moment with this lunar pairing – lots of excitement and passion. You share a yearning for adventure.

CAPRICORN – This lunar pairing is best suited to business relationships, but there is no bar to an intimate one as long as you remember to apply common sense.

AQUARIUS – If you are both prepared to respect each other's need for independence all will be well with this mix of Moons.

PISCES – It is doubtful if a person with an

'Boys and girls come out to play, The moon doth shine as bright as day.'

Nursery Rhyme

Aries Moon has the necessary patience for this pairing to become a lasting relationship. A Pisces Moon person is too sensitive for you.

IF YOUR MOON IS IN TAURUS
and your partner has their Moon in…

ARIES – You may be worried by your partner's impulsiveness and long for a little more security.

TAURUS – Your emotional advantages and needs are exactly the same so you should have few grounds for disagreement.

GEMINI – A wayward lunar Gemini wouldn't suit a lunar Taurean whose basic need is for stability in their life.

CANCER – This is a very loving and supportive combination. You should be happy with each other's emotional natures.

LEO – Both Taurus and Leo are stubborn fixed signs so there will be the odd clash of wills. Apart from that you should generally get on.

VIRGO – This is a compatible mix. The lunar Virgo will love your common sense and steadfastness. You love lunar Virgo's mind, and you two have a good sexual relationship.

LIBRA – Two such creative signs can't fail to get along. Your relationship should be loving and sensual.

SCORPIO – This will be either heaven or hell. You may both be too stubborn or else you may be extremely supportive of each other.

SAGITTARIUS – This has the makings of a terrible mess. Your emotional viewpoints are too diverse for anything lasting.

CAPRICORN – This is a splendid combination physically, emotionally and mentally, with all the makings of a stable relationship.

AQUARIUS – There may be some meeting of minds, but Aquarian eccentricity will eventually wear out a lunar Taurean.

PISCES – The lunar Taurean will give the lunar Piscean emotional strength while your partner will give you unstinting affection.

IF YOUR MOON IS IN GEMINI
and your partner has their Moon in…

ARIES – There may be some disagreements, but on the whole you will be in tune with your partner.

TAURUS – The steady ways of the lunar Taurean will be a little *too* steady for you. You need more variety.

*'The dark plains on the lunar surface
are still called seas, even though the Moon
could not support liquid water. '*

GEMINI – Both of you will be too fickle for the relationship to last long, but it will be fun while it's happening!

CANCER – The possessiveness of the lunar Cancerian will appal the flighty Gemini Moon.

LEO – This should be a fun combination with plenty of laughs. Just remember that a lunar Leo has a super-sensitive ego.

VIRGO – You may have plenty of interests in common, but there is not enough emotional stability to ensure a permanent union between you two.

LIBRA – This link-up has the potential of being marvellous. Compatible signs give a mutual appreciation.

SCORPIO – As long as jealousy doesn't overwhelm your finer feelings, this match should be sexually sizzling.

SAGITTARIUS – You've got a lot in common with the lunar Sagittarian and you should have the ability to understand each other instinctively.

CAPRICORN – You have a vast difference in emotional needs and viewpoint. This partnership could be difficult to maintain.

AQUARIUS – Getting along together should be easy. You'll love your partner's mind and independent attitudes.

PISCES – The constant need for emotional support from a lunar Piscean will irritate a Gemini Moon.

IF YOUR MOON IS IN CANCER
and your partner has their Moon in...

ARIES – You'll need more comforting and affection than a lunar Aries is likely to give.

TAURUS – Your affectionate ways will find a compatible match in a lunar Taurean.

GEMINI – The flighty lunar Gemini nature will set your teeth on edge. This is not a likely match.

CANCER – This relationship will work because you will both be in tune with each other. This should be cosy and traditional.

LEO – If you are prepared to take a back seat and praise your partner, then this match should just work.

VIRGO – Your strong emotions and protective instincts will please the lunar Virgo while your partner's logical mind will be invaluable to you.

LIBRA – You may find the lunar Libran too cool and refined for your taste. He or she might find you too demanding.

SCORPIO – This is a compatible match with strong emotions and intense expressions of heartfelt passion.

SAGITTARIUS – You will never truly understand a lunar Sagittarian, and he or she will never, ever understand you. You might be compatible as friends, though.

CAPRICORN – Although you won't have much common ground, this partnership can nevertheless work.

AQUARIUS – The independent lunar Aquarian doesn't need the clinging Cancerian type and vice versa.

PISCES – A very compatible link if both Moons are in these gentle water signs. This will make a loving relationship.

IF YOUR MOON IS IN LEO

and your partner has their Moon in…

ARIES – This could be a match made in heaven as long as you don't offend your partner's ego and they don't get in your way.

TAURUS – You are both stubborn, but with just enough leeway to make a lasting love link.

GEMINI – This should be an exciting mix, with just the occasional clash of wills to keep it all interesting.

CANCER – If you can restrain yourself from calling all the shots, then this link could conceivably work.

LEO – Two big egos need a lot of room to express themselves, yet you will have identical needs.

VIRGO – You won't like the constant analysis of the lunar Virgo. You need something more spontaneous and fun.

LIBRA – If you are looking for the high life, then team up with a lunar Libran to form a mutual admiration society made specifically for two.

SCORPIO – With a lunar Scorpio you'll find an instant magnetic attraction. Sexually passionate, you'll have to work on the other areas.

SAGITTARIUS – This is a perfectly compatible mixture because these fire signs get along. This should be a vigorous love affair.

CAPRICORN – You will have to be magnanimous and forgiving because a person with a

Capricorn Moon will easily bruise your ego.

AQUARIUS – You may see the world through very different eyes but in many ways your contrasts add charm to your relationship.

PISCES – This could be a softly romantic liaison. There's a kind of magic that will win your heart.

IF YOUR MOON IS IN VIRGO
and your partner has their Moon in…

ARIES – The sudden passions and enthusiasms of your partner could distress you.

TAURUS – Both lunar signs have a great deal in common and make a compatible match for lasting happiness.

GEMINI – There is plenty of intellectual stimulation in this pairing, but you still will have many differences.

CANCER – Each partner seems to have what the other needs so this is a mutually beneficial partnership.

LEO – Bolstering your Leo Moon partner's sensitive ego may wear you out.

VIRGO – As with all same-sign matches, there's plenty in common but pitfalls too. You may be unable to relax fully.

LIBRA – This is a great match for friendship, conversations and artistic appreciation, but the passion may be wanting.

SCORPIO – This is an extremely passionate combination, giving you a chance to let your hair down.

SAGITTARIUS – The wayward lunar Sagittarian nature may disturb lunar Virgos yet there is come common ground, even if you have to give a little.

CAPRICORN – This is a combination that truly understands each other. You will both be comfortable, but must make an effort to inject excitement.

AQUARIUS – This is a strange mix of the precise and the unpredictable. Both of you must be prepared to give and take.

PISCES – The overly sentimental Pisces Moon person will find little emotional support from the lunar Virgo. You are probably best as friends.

IF YOUR MOON IS IN LIBRA
and your partner has their Moon in….

ARIES – Impatience is the main problem in this pairing. You need time to ponder, whereas the lunar Aries demands instant results.

TAURUS – This should be a refined match

> *'The moon is nothing*
> *But a circumambulatory*
> *aphrodisiac*
> *Divinely subsidized to*
> *provoke the world*
> *Into a rising birth-rate.'*
>
> Christopher Fry,
> *The Dark is Light Enough*

with more than a hint of sensuality. You will have much in common.

GEMINI – Since both Gemini and Libra are 'airy' signs this is a compatible mixture. You will tend to love the same things.

CANCER – You may find yourself worn down by the lunar Cancerian's constant need for your attention.

LEO – If you want a life filled with luxury, then team up with a lunar Leo. The credit card bills are likely to be horrendous, however.

VIRGO – This is a good team for friendship, but in the passion stakes you both seem to desire different things.

LIBRA – You have much in common, including your indecision. The danger is that you might never get anything done.

SCORPIO – Lunar Scorpios can be very demanding, which may be too much to cope with when you have a delicate Libran Moon.

SAGITTARIUS – If you are prepared to give your partner a little space then this combination could just work.

CAPRICORN – The frivolity of the Libran Moon may not find much common ground with the staid lunar Capricorn.

AQUARIUS – This will be a good match with both of you finding pleasure in each other's company. You'll have lots of fun and an understanding relationship.

PISCES – Love, commitment and sensuality are on offer in this match. However, you may be rather judgemental of each other's faults.

IF YOUR MOON IS IN SCORPIO

and your partner has their Moon in…

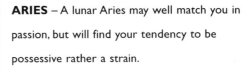

ARIES – A lunar Aries may well match you in passion, but will find your tendency to be possessive rather a strain.

TAURUS – This mixture of Moon signs can be very creative and successful, even though you will have very different viewpoints.

GEMINI – Freedom is important to a lunar Gemini, so your tendency to be possessive could create problems within the relationship.

CANCER – Although a temperamental mix, lunar Cancerians and Scorpios are highly compatible. Intense passion is likely.

LEO – On the surface this may seem to be a quarrelsome mix, yet there is a volcanic attraction between the two of you.

VIRGO – Lunar Scorpio sex-drive meets Virgo earthiness in an intense relationship, but try not to be too demanding.

LIBRA – The indecision of a Libran Moon will irritate a lunar Scorpio who demands

total devotion from their partner.

SCORPIO – This relationship will find you either too alike for comfort or open rivals. It all depends on how you are prepared to play it.

SAGITTARIUS – You may find that the lunar Sagittarian's freedom-loving ways do not provide the stability you need.

CAPRICORN – This is a good mix, though you must allow each other the freedom to follow your own destinies.

AQUARIUS – You may find someone with an Aquarian Moon to be too cool and aloof for your passionate nature.

PISCES – Your two signs are very compatible and you will find yourselves irresistibly attracted. You'll even have a soft spot for each other's weaknesses.

IF YOUR MOON IS IN SAGITTARIUS
and your partner has their Moon in...

ARIES – These two hot signs get on like a proverbial house on fire. Equally, tempers will occasionally flair. Never a dull moment.

TAURUS – You will find a Taurus Moon person too staid and dull, while lunar Taureans will not find the stability they crave.

GEMINI – Gemini is opposite Sagittarius in the zodiac and this combination of lunar signs can indeed make for a lasting love link.

CANCER – There is very little scope for understanding between the freedom-loving nature of the lunar Sagittarian and the domestic virtues of the lunar Cancerian.

LEO – This is an extremely good mix: interesting, fun and exciting. These two fire signs can get along just fine.

VIRGO – The independent attitudes of both Virgo and Sagittarius make this an unlikely match, yet as friends you are ideal.

LIBRA – A respect for each other's privacy will go a long way to making this relationship work.

SCORPIO – The natures of Scorpio and Sagittarius are so different to ensure that there will be little common ground in this mix.

SAGITTARIUS – You obviously will be very alike in your needs but may actually spend little time together.

CAPRICORN – This mix could be very difficult. You both see the world with different eyes so will have little agreement.

AQUARIUS – This relationship will break all the rules and that is what gives it its sense of adventure.

PISCES – You may find a lunar Piscean too dependent for comfort, yet come to respect the unstinting affection your partner can give.

IF YOUR MOON IS IN CAPRICORN

and your partner has their Moon in...

ARIES – A relationship between these two Moon signs is better suited to a business arrangement rather than a personal one.

TAURUS – These two earthy signs are perfectly compatible. You will understand each other deeply.

GEMINI – There are fundamental differences in your emotional make-up that will make agreement difficult to achieve.

CANCER – Cancer is the opposite sign to Capricorn and if your respective Moons are in these signs a deep understanding will develop.

LEO – The extravagance of the Leo Moon person will appal the thrifty lunar Capricorn. Likewise, the truthful lunar Capricorn will easily wound the lunar Leo.

VIRGO – A good chance of a lasting love link occurs when these two earthy signs are occupied by your respective Moons.

LIBRA – You may be too hard on your Libran Moon lover. Try to be more gentle, as they are not made of such stern stuff as you.

SCORPIO – Sexually, this should be a great union. In other ways too there will be a mutual respect.

SAGITTARIUS – The lunar Sagittarian's flights of fancy will irritate the realistic Capricorn Moon personality.

CAPRICORN – It's likely that you are both career-minded and the two of you will be able to forge a lasting bond based on such practical concerns.

AQUARIUS – A lunar Aquarian can cheer you up when you are in one of your despondent phases. A few surprises can be a positive thing.

PISCES – The soft, sentimental lunar Piscean nature will not find favour with your hard-headed approach to love.

> *'Late, late yestreen I saw the new moon, Wi' the auld moon in her arm.'*
>
> Ballad of *Sir Patrick Spens*

'The word "lunatic" literally means "afflicted by the Moon". This comes from the belief that the Moon governs madmen and poets.'

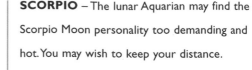

IF YOUR MOON IS IN AQUARIUS
and your partner has their Moon in…

ARIES – Both Aries and Aquarius are known as go-ahead, independent signs so with your respective Moons you will develop mutual respect and admiration.

TAURUS – The lunar Aquarian will be too eccentric and freedom-loving for the average lunar Taurean.

GEMINI – This is a compatible mix of air signs. You will see the world in similar terms and get on in an odd sort of way.

CANCER – A lunar Aquarian cannot truly fulfil the emotional needs of the Cancer Moon personality.

LEO – Aquarius and Leo are opposite signs yet have much in common. This partnership can work surprisingly well.

VIRGO – Both signs are cool and independent so there will be a meeting of minds … will hearts and bodies follow?

LIBRA – These two signs have much in common and a mutual understanding would be easy if only the lunar Aquarian could fulfil the lunar Libran's need for romance.

SCORPIO – The lunar Aquarian may find the Scorpio Moon personality too demanding and hot. You may wish to keep your distance.

SAGITTARIUS – This is a good mix in which you will mutually understand each other's need for freedom.

CAPRICORN – There isn't a great deal in common in ways of thinking, yet you can lighten a lunar Capricorn's mood.

AQUARIUS – All bets are off. This mix can be marvellous or absolute hell. The prospect of two lunar Aquarians together is an unpredictable proposition.

PISCES – You will never truly understand each other, yet for many, regarding each other as enigmas will actually strengthen your union.

IF YOUR MOON IS IN PISCES
and your partner has their Moon in…

ARIES – The abrupt lunar Aries manner will upset your sensitive Pisces Moon personality.

TAURUS – The lunar Piscean could do with some good, old-fashioned lunar Taurean practicality. You two should get on.

GEMINI – The lunar Gemini will make you laugh, then very probably cry. You will never understand each other's feelings.

CANCER – A perfectly compatible partnership is possible with this pairing of watery signs. You will be extremely affectionate.

LEO – Since both Leo and Pisces adore romance this combination could just work on an emotional level.

VIRGO – Virgo is the opposite sign to Pisces and though there will be irritations this is a match that can work with mutual respect.

LIBRA – Both of you are lovers of beauty, refinement, art and the finer things of life. You have a lot of common ground.

SCORPIO – This is a perfect match of watery signs. Emotionally in tune, the intensity of your passions will make you feel more secure.

SAGITTARIUS – There is some common ground intellectually between these two signs, but a lunar Sagittarian's ways may make you feel somewhat unnecessary.

CAPRICORN – There is little sympathy here. A lunar Capricorn will be too hard on your sensitive Piscean Moon personality.

AQUARIUS – This is a peculiar mix in which both partners will regard the other as something of a mystery. This probably means neither of you will ever be bored.

PISCES – You are both soft, gentle, sentimental and constantly trying to make the other take the lead. This might lead nowhere or develop into a deep spiritual union.

REVEALING YOUR DEEPER PERSONALITY

•

Your rising sign reveals the situation you were born into and the influences you experienced as a child.

REVEALING YOUR DEEPER PERSONALITY

•

WHAT IS A RISING SIGN?

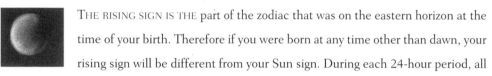 THE RISING SIGN IS THE part of the zodiac that was on the eastern horizon at the time of your birth. Therefore if you were born at any time other than dawn, your rising sign will be different from your Sun sign. During each 24-hour period, all 12 zodiac signs rise over this point. Your Sun sign depends upon the time of year in which you were born, your Moon sign depends upon the position of the Moon at the time you were born, but your rising sign depends upon the time of birth on that particular day. Only someone who was born within minutes of yourself will have the same combination.

Your rising sign shows the situation that you were born into and the programming that you were subjected to as a child from parents, school teachers, friends and society at the time and place of your birth. We are all taught to behave in a certain way, which often results in our outer behaviour being more like our rising sign than our Sun sign. The rising sign can also account for the differences in appearance between people of the same Sun sign.

Use the Rising Sign wheel to find your own rising sign. The first step is to find your time of birth on the outer circle. You will notice that this is in hour segments, but if you look closely you will see that you can find your time to the nearest half hour. (*NB* Use the birth time as you know it and don't adjust for British Summer Time or Daylight Saving.)

'It is considered good luck to move house when the Moon is waning because superstition asserts that you will never go hungry.'

Look at the inner wheel and locate your Sun Sign, then align this to your time of birth. For instance, if you were a Sagittarian who was born at 10.30am, place the Sagittarian arrow in the 10.30am section.

Now look to the wheel where you see the words 'Rising Sign' on the outer wheel. The sign that is closest to the mark will be your rising sign. It is Aquarius. You may find that the rising sign marker lies between two signs, and in this case read about both signs to see which fits you best. If you are doubtful about your exact time of birth or your exact rising sign, read the one that is marked before and after yours on the wheel and you will soon recognize the one that relates to you.

> 'To rake the moon from out the sea.
> The bowl goes trim. The moon doth shine,
> And our ballast is old wine.'
>
> T. L. Peacock, *Three Men of Gotham*

If you want absolute accuracy then you must visit a consultant astrologer and you must have accurate data for your date, time and place of birth.

Next, read through the character descriptions that follow to discover more about yourself. If you are not sure which of two signs you have rising, read both profiles and decide which suits you best. Try this system out on your family and friends to understand more about their behaviour.

●

YOUR RISING SIGN PROFILE

ARIES RISING

You might think that having this fire sign rising would make you an extrovert, but it doesn't necessarily. You can be quiet, cautious and also slightly shy, and you can even come across to others as a touch hostile until they get to know you better. You may feel you had a difficult relationship with your parents, especially your father, who you might have seen as dictatorial and prone to disagree with you and put you down. Your family may have moved around from one place to another, giving you a rather unsettled school life. A family background with a formal kind of organization is possible, as is a strongly religious background, which you may have felt to be too hidebound or regulated. Any of these childhood difficulties could lead to difficult relationships later in life.

'If you want to perform any magic, the waxing Moon is a good time in which to get results, but the Full Moon is even better. '

If there was no shortage of intellectual stimulation around the parental home, you would have been given plenty of opportunities to study and to achieve.

TAURUS RISING

If you believe that money and possessions are extremely important, this is likely to have come out of the experiences of your childhood. Even if your childhood home was conventional and comfortable, there may have been a strong emphasis on getting on in life and on saving for a rainy day. Your parents may have been stingy, or conversely they could have been spendthrift, but the results are the same. In adulthood, you feel that you need a large house and plenty of material things in order to feel comfortable. One benefit of this is that you can create a beautiful home, and you may even turn your talents to money-making use later in life.

Your relationships with others can veer between being extremely harmonious and confrontational. If you suffer from feelings of jealousy, this may well hark back to the 'keep hold of everything that comes your way' messages that you absorbed during your childhood.

GEMINI RISING

A situation may have arisen during your childhood, either at home or at school, which made you feel like a square peg in a round hole. Some Gemini rising people have a terrible time in childhood, and this can be due to extremely difficult family circumstances – for instance, you may have been brought up by people who were not your natural parents and who did so out of

'The waning Moon is a poor time for any magical work, as negative results may ensue.'

duty or on sufferance. Even if your home life was fine, you may not have fitted in well at school. One reason for this could be that you were very quick and bright, even as a small child, and this will have put other children's backs up. Being a good communicator is a useful talent for an adult, but most teachers really want a child who is seen and not heard. In later life you may be able to put your communications skills to good use; you are sympathetic to others who also don't fit in and who find life difficult.

CANCER RISING

If you were the oldest child in your family, or were the one who assumed the most responsibility, to some extent you had an old head on your shoulders when you were young. You may have also been blessed with a rather maternal father, to whom you felt close, and a happy and comfortable home life. Another possibility is that your mother was a strong personality who held the family together during hard times, and could be perceived as domineering or frightening or as very loving. This might have left you with a great deal of love and admiration for your mother, but also, deep down, possibly some buried fear and anger. Later in life, you have all the qualities to make an excellent parent, a reliable employee and a shrewd business person.

LEO RISING

A child with Leo rising is most likely a wanted child, and your parents may have considered you to be special in some way – indeed you may have been a talented child. There is a strong sense of the dramatic, and many are drawn to the stage, or at the very least will take a prominent role in whatever situation they find themselves. Other people will be attracted to their slightly 'larger than life' expressions of personality. However, there will also be some who will resent the easy manner and flamboyant style of the Leo rising person. Remember that the natural place for someone who possesses this configuration is centre stage. Basking in the limelight is as natural as breathing, so if the less talented are envious than it should be taken as a sort of back-handed compliment. After all, a person with Leo rising is not likely to be petty minded and will easily rise above all criticism.

VIRGO RISING

This rising sign doesn't always make for an easy passage during childhood. Some Virgo rising children find themselves compared unfavourably with others in the family, or you may have got on well with one parent or sibling whilst finding it difficult to get on with the others.

As an adult you can be intelligent and also mentally well-organized, which means that you are admirably suited to academic work, research projects or anything that needs analyzing and filing away in its proper place. However, you can be shy and mistrustful, and therefore slow to form love relationships.

LIBRA RISING

If you came into the world with a silver spoon in your mouth, you may rarely have to put yourself to a great deal of trouble to get what you want, as there are people around who are only too happy to help you out. It is possible that your father may have done a disappearing act early on, or he may not have been at home much; if so, when he was around, he may have indulged you with toys in compensation for his lack of any real interest. If you were close to your mother, this could also mean that she spoiled or indulged you.

Oddly enough, such a scenario could lead you to leave home and to marry at an early age. The motivation for this could be a need to strike out on your own away from your family. Those with a 'charmed life' seem to find that relationships and work don't usually turn out to be difficult.

'A savage place! as holy
and enchanted
As e'er beneath a waning
moon was haunted
By woman wailing for her
demon lover!'

S. T. Coleridge, *Kubla Khan*

SCORPIO RISING

For all that this is such an intense sign, it does not necessarily mean that you have had a head start in life. Your parents may have loved you and done their best to look after you, but there could have been awkward relationships between yourself and your brothers, sisters or other family members. Another problem is that you may not have quite fitted in with the other children at your school – your parents probably could do little to help you, and eventually you would have given up complaining and kept your feelings to yourself. In later life, if you continue to keep your true feelings close to your chest, this can make you difficult for others to understand.

SAGITTARIUS RISING

People with this configuration can be cheerful, outgoing and popular, with a great sense of humour. At the same time, you may be very interested in mind, body and spirit subjects such as astrology, or some other philosophical or religious type of thinking. Although your childhood may have been pretty ordinary with nothing for you to complain about, your parents might have come from a culture or a religious background that you possibly feel no longer serves its purpose for the time and place in which you live. If so, this could lead you to turn away from your parents' beliefs and work out your own.

You may be known for your honesty and generosity, and you can get on well with most people that you meet. However, you are quite likely to be a bit off-beat or different, which means that you often choose your friends and colleagues from among those with similar outlook and tastes to yourself.

CAPRICORN RISING

You may have been loved and wanted as a child, but your family's circumstances during your childhood could have been far from perfect. Your family may have been desperately short of money or labouring under difficulties of some other kind. If so, messages about hard work and good savings schemes might have been picked up by you very early on. If you were an elder child in a large household your parents might have had little time to devote to you. Being shy and quiet, you may not have made a great splash at school, and in this case you would have gone your way quietly, with an old head on your young shoulders and little to really enjoy in life.

Later on, if you do well in your job or you make money in business, you may do your best to help your parents and brothers and sisters, thus making it possible for the whole family to enjoy a better lifestyle and happier times as the years go by.

> HIPPOLYTA: *'I am weary of this moon, would that he would change.'*
> THESEUS: *'It appears, by his small light of discretion, that he is on the wane.'*
>
> William Shakespeare,
> *A Midsummer's Night Dream*

AQUARIUS RISING

Either your childhood was a happy and relaxed affair or it was something of a nightmare – there doesn't seem to be a middle road here. If you were happy at home and at school, you could have enjoyed playing with friends and doing out-of-school activities. If there was trouble in the house, it could have been because you couldn't get on with one or other of your parents. A tendency to outspokenness can upset parents – and it may not endear you to school teachers either. Whatever your childhood was like, if you had access to books, music and education, you may have put this to good use in your later working life.

The chances are that although you may have left home early in order to make your own way, your later lifestyle will be quite conventional.

PISCES RISING

If you spent a fair amount of your childhood alone, there can be any number of reasons for this: perhaps you were ill during childhood, or you might simply have been fond of your own company. If this was the case, it may be that you simply didn't fit in with those around you. This mental or physical isolation could have set you off on an inward journey so that you began to explore spiritual and metaphysical ideas. Your imagination may have been stimulated by reading and listening to music, and all this could well turn you towards an artistic, musical or spiritual lifestyle as an adult. You can be hugely sympathetic to those in need, and you may be leaned on by freeloaders if you are not careful.

'Traditionally, an eclipse is said to foretell the loss of a friend or lover, an unfaithful partner or the onset of poverty.'

UNDERSTANDING THE ASTROLOGICAL HOUSES

You will see that the Astrological Houses wheel in the pocket has 12 'segments' around the rim: Image, Wealth, Travel, Home, Pleasure, Health, Relationships, Sex, Spirituality, Career, Friendships and Secrets. These segments represent the 12 astrological houses. Each house represents a different area of one's life, so when you put your solar and lunar horoscope together you will see how your signs influence the nature of your Sun and Moon, and how your houses direct the energies of these planets. Bearing in mind that the Moon exerts a strong influence on your inner desires rather than the outer solar influences of family, friends, culture and society, it is the sign and house of the Moon that will show your real inner needs.

'To dream of the Moon is an omen of unexpected joy and success. A Full Moon will reveal marriage or prosperity for a widow.'

HOW TO USE THE WHEEL

Align your rising sign with the 'house' marked 1, Image, then put a little piece of sticking paper, or use a child's felt tip pen that can be rubbed off afterwards, to make a dot in the sign that your natal Moon is in. Now you can see the 'house' that your Moon sign is in. For example, if you are Gemini rising and your Moon is in Pisces, your Moon is in the tenth house of career, so write this down and look up its interpretation on page 74.

AN EXAMPLE OF INTERPRETATION

A successful career person may have his Moon in Cancer in the second house. This might mean he has a secret desire to spend his days restoring antique furniture or growing orchids rather than going out to a busy office day after day. This is because Cancer is associated with the home and its surroundings and also with historical or antique objects, while the second house is associated with things of beauty and value, plus farming and gardening. It is often only when the family has grown up and one's working life is over that such inner dreams and desires can actually be fulfilled.

> *'The white saucer like some full moon descends At last from the clouds of the table above.'*
>
> Harold Monro,
> *Milk for the Cat*

THE FIRST HOUSE – **Image and the Self**

This house belongs to you yourself and, being so close to the rising sign, it emphasizes the programming you received in childhood. It is associated with your appearance, manner and image. This house can show talents and abilities and to some extent the kind of career or lifestyle that suits you.

THE SECOND HOUSE – **Wealth, Personal Values and Priorities**

This house is concerned with valued personal possessions and personal finances, plus your basic needs of food, clothing and shelter. Self-esteem and the way you value yourself, and to some extent other relationships are ruled by this house. Abstract priorities such as time, security, love and freedom can be shown by the sign that this house occupies.

THE THIRD HOUSE – **Travel and Communications**

This house is associated with brothers, sisters, cousins, neighbours and close friendships. It rules communications and information of all kinds, including paperwork, negotiations and figurework. The way you think and express yourself, your basic education and your level of dexterity are shown here. Local travel, short journeys and your chosen mode of transport are ruled by this house.

THE FOURTH HOUSE – **Home and Family**

This house rules the parents, especially the mother or mother figure, and it concerns the childhood home, the start you got in life and how your life will progress. The fourth house is also associated with your domestic circumstances throughout your life, your home, land and

'To travel by land, choose the increase of the Moon. Choose the decrease of the Moon for a voyage.'

property or your business premises. It is mainly associated with all kinds of family matters. The past, antiques, history and patriotism are found here.

THE FIFTH HOUSE – **Pleasure, Creativity and Leisure**

This house covers artistry and creativity, especially music. The creation of a family (especially children), a business enterprise, a work of art or a book are found here. This house is associated with pleasure, holidays, hobbies and games that are fun and amusing. Fun-filled love affairs, plus the love of children and pets are associated with the fifth house, as is time off from the realities of daily life.

THE SIXTH HOUSE – **Health and Work**

This house rules employers and employees, work and duty of all kinds. It traditionally ruled the harvest, but nowadays this can mean all that you have worked for over a period of time. Health, prevention of illness and anything to do with fitness are indicated here.

THE SEVENTH HOUSE – **Relationships**

Traditionally, this is the house of marriage, but nowadays it can rule any close partnership that is open and above board, including business partnerships. Open relationships can include your enemies! The seventh house also rules agreements, contracts and justice.

THE EIGHTH HOUSE – **Sex, Union, Separation and Finances**

This is concerned with shared finances and resources, which might be personal or business. It also rules dealings with financial institutions, legacies, taxes, corporate matters and even the police or judiciary. Birth, death, sex and karma are associated with this house, as are secrets and hidden or occult matters.

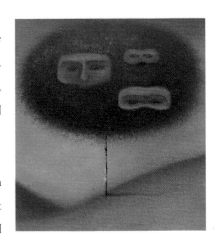

THE NINTH HOUSE – **Spirituality, Exploration and Expansion**

Long-distance travel or dealings with foreigners, foreign goods or different cultures of all kinds are associated with this house. Issues of freedom and

independence and ways of pushing back boundaries are ruled by the ninth house. Anything that expands one's intellectual horizons, such as higher education, religion or philosophy, are found here, as is anything related to the law. Gambling, especially on horses, is traditionally associated with this house.

THE TENTH HOUSE – **Career and Ambition**

This house is often taken to mean one's career, but it really represents any kind of goal or ambition. Parents, especially father figures, are ruled here, as are authority figures of all kinds. Status, public acclaim, political advancement and anything else that happens outside the home and/or in the public eye are ruled by this house.

THE ELEVENTH HOUSE – **Friendships, Groups, Hopes and Wishes**

This house rules detached relationships such as one finds in clubs, societies and group activities, and all manner of acquaintances or loose friendships. Education, the acquisition of knowledge and original or unusual ideas are associated with this house. Intellectual pastimes and astrology can be found here. Your hopes and wishes are ruled by this house.

THE TWELFTH HOUSE – **Secrets, Sacrifice and Seclusion**

This house rules sacrifice and caring for the weak. It also concerns self-undoing and unhealthy forms of escapism, such as drinking too much. Places of seclusion, such as prisons and hospitals, are attached to this house. Mysticism, the hidden sides of life, secrets and feelings of insecurity are kept here. Planets in this house often lend artistry, musical talent or psychic ability to the subject.

'Plant your vegetables during the "fruitful" water signs of Cancer, Scorpio and Pisces. Gemini, Leo, Virgo and Aries are said to be barren times.'

THE MOON IN DIFFERENT HOUSES

THE MOON IN THE FIRST HOUSE

If your Moon is in the first house, you will be strongly affected by your mother, whether for good or for ill. Perhaps it is your mother's circumstances or position in life that impinge upon you. Your emotions are strong and sensitive, but depending upon the type of sign aligned with this house, these may be repressed or openly expressed. You will be restless, fond of travel and the sea, and you may live or work by water. Family life will be important to you, and you may seek out a maternal partner in life.

THE MOON IN THE SECOND HOUSE

You need security and you will save for what you want. You may collect goods, money, antiques or *objets d'art*. You have excellent business instincts, but your luck ebbs and flows. Your feelings towards those you love are strong, and you may be prone to jealousy or possessiveness.

THE MOON IN THE THIRD HOUSE

You are very attached to brothers, sisters, relatives, friends and neighbours. You need to feel attached to a neighbourhood. You take responsibility for other family members. Your early education may have been disrupted and you need to learn to concentrate. You may be interested in journalism or writing.

THE MOON IN THE FOURTH HOUSE

You might be clingy, maternal and home-loving. You may need more love than can reasonably be given. You may enjoy working from home or with children in a home-like atmosphere. You may be interested in history, stamp-collecting or items from the past.

THE MOON IN THE FIFTH HOUSE

You are outgoing and rather dramatic in your approach to love and life. You may want a glamorous lifestyle, possibly in fashion, the arts, the

*'If the Sun and Moon
should doubt,
They'd immediately
go out.'*

William Blake,
Auguries of Innocence

stage or sports. You could fill your life with children, or you could be too frivolous to ever grow up yourself. Love affairs are seen as fun.

THE MOON IN THE SIXTH HOUSE

You may have been ill during childhood, or you could be obsessed by health, hygiene, food and fitness. You may work from home or move house due to work. You may have had a demanding mother – or you may be one yourself. You can express yourself by writing.

THE MOON IN THE SEVENTH HOUSE

You may be vulnerable and dependent, needing a maternal partner, but you can also seek to smother or control others. You are exceptionally interested in business matters and you make successful working partnerships.

THE MOON IN THE EIGHTH HOUSE

You are keen on psychic or intuitive topics and you have strong ESP. Sex is an issue in your life, and you may even become preoccupied with it. You could become involved in public finances or you could be strongly influenced by a partner's financial position. You have a talent for business.

THE MOON IN THE NINTH HOUSE

You are attracted to spiritual subjects and you may take an interest in a variety of them. You may be good at languages and you could travel to or live in a variety of countries. You may marry a foreigner. You have wide-ranging interests such as ecology, animals, legal matters and politics. You may write or broadcast.

THE MOON IN THE TENTH HOUSE

You take your career or your public standing and status very seriously. You may be drawn to politics or public service, and this can lead you to ignore your private life. Alternatively, your family may be in the public eye and you could achieve wealth or fame at second hand. Business and success are important to you.

THE MOON IN THE ELEVENTH HOUSE

You may be cool and detached and not really keen on close personal relationships. You prefer friends, clubs, group activities or business to family life. Your objectives in life may be particuliar, or they may change from one month to the next.

THE MOON IN THE TWELFTH HOUSE

You need time to get over childhood problems or your feelings towards your parents or other family members. You could learn hard lessons through family life. You may appear tough, but you are vulnerable and sensitive. Under stress you may become ill, or you may take to drink or drugs. On the plus side, you are highly intuitive and extremely creative and artistic. You are kind-hearted, and you make and keep good friends.

•

THE ASTROLOGICAL HOUSES AND YOUR HEALTH

The Moon relates to your emotional nature and, as we all know, emotional stress and unhappiness can result in diseases or health problems of one sort or another. Oddly enough accidents can trigger off illnesses because they are sudden and unexpected, and can bring a great deal of stress in their wake. In the case of an accident, it is not usually stress and emotional pain that brings on the ailment, but the stress of the pain and immobilization which follows the accident.

THE MOON AND PARTS OF THE BODY – Each house of the zodiac is associated with a different part of the body so knowing which house your Moon is in can show you which part of the body is likely to let you down.

MOON IN THE FIRST HOUSE OF IMAGE – affects the head, brain, eyes, skull and upper jaw and upper teeth; also the pineal gland and the arteries to the head and brain.

MOON IN THE SECOND HOUSE OF WEALTH – affects the lower jaw and upper teeth, the throat (including the thyroid gland), the neck, larynx, chin, ears, tongue, vocal cords, the upper (cervical) spine, the jugular vein, the tonsils.

MOON IN THE THIRD HOUSE OF TRAVEL – affects the upper respiratory system, the shoulders, arms, wrists, hands and fingers, and the upper ribs.

MOON IN THE FOURTH HOUSE OF HOME – affects the lungs, breasts, ribcage, stomach and digestive organs, alimentary canal, sternum, womb and pancreas.

MOON IN THE FIFTH HOUSE OF PLEASURE – affects the spine (especially the upper back), the spinal cord, the heart, the arteries (especially the aorta), the circulation, the spleen.

MOON IN THE SIXTH HOUSE OF HEALTH – affects the lower digestive system, the bowels, the lower dorsal nerves, the nervous system and the mind.

MOON IN THE SEVENTH HOUSE OF RELATIONSHIPS – affects the bladder, kidneys, lumbar region, haunches to buttocks, adrenal glands, lumbar nerves and blood vessels.

MOON IN THE EIGHTH HOUSE OF SEX – affects the reproductive and sexual organs (especially the cervix), the lower stomach, the lower spine including the coccyx, the groin, anus, genito-urinary system and prostate gland. This house may, like the first, relate to the eyes.

'The Moon is said to be the heavenly abode of the archangel Gabriel, who is most commonly shown wearing silver robes.'

MOON IN THE NINTH HOUSE OF SPIRITUALITY – affects the hips and thighs, the pelvis, the sacrum, the liver, the sciatic nerve and arterial system, especially the femoral arteries.

MOON IN THE TENTH HOUSE OF CAREER – affects the skin, ears, teeth, bones and knees.

MOON IN THE ELEVENTH HOUSE OF FRIENDSHIPS – affects the ankles, calves and shins, breathing and the circulatory system – especially to the extremeties.

> 'Soon as the evening shades prevail,
> The moon takes up the wondrous tale,
> And nightly to the listening earth
> Repeats the story of her birth:
> Whilst all the stars that round
> her burn,
> And all the planets in their turn,
> Confirm the tidings as they roll,
> And spread the truth from pole to pole.'
>
> Joseph Addison, *The Spectator*

MOON IN THE TWELFTH HOUSE OF SECRETS – affects the feet and toes, lungs, lymphatic system and pituitary gland. The mind can be upset by psychic phenomena or by the angry or disturbed emotions of others around you.

DISCOVERING YOUR MOON HOROSCOPE

•

The cycle of the Moon
influences events throughout
your life, as well as your feelings,
moods and emotions.

THE CYCLE OF THE MOON

•

THE PHASES OF THE MOON

THE MOON PASSES THROUGH eight major phases during its 28-day cycle. These are New, Waxing Crescent, First Quarter, Waxing Gibbous or Misshaped, Full, Waning Gibbous, Last Quarter, and Old or Waning Crescent. The most important of these are, of course, the New and Full Moons, which are dealt with on the following pages.

NEW MOON	FULL MOON
(See opposite. Take note of the sign and house of the New Moon.)	(See page 85. Take note of the sign and house of the Full Moon.)

THE WAXING CRESCENT occurs three days after the New Moon. It represents a discussion of new ideas. Sociability comes into focus.

THE FIRST QUARTER occurs seven days after the New Moon and is a time for settlements and conclusions. Home life is very important now.

THE WAXING GIBBOUS MOON starts three to four days before the Moon is full. It could be a time of laziness or at least of forced efforts.

THE WANING GIBBOUS MOON follows the Full Moon by three to four days. Emotions run high, ranging from euphoria to despondency. You need to talk things over.

THE LAST QUARTER occurs seven days after Full Moon. It adds to responsibilities. Time may be wasted by complainers.

THE OLD MOON OR WANING CRESCENT is also called the Dark of the Moon. This is the time for secrets and subtlety. Clear something negative from your life now.

THE NEW MOON

THE NEW MOON IN THE SIGNS

The New Moon in Aries can give a quick temper, but also powers of leadership and great initiative.

The New Moon in Taurus gives stamina, patience and stubborn purpose. This is good for financial planning.

The New Moon in Gemini gives persuasion and versatility. This is an ingenious influence, but may be flippant.

The New Moon in Cancer favours domesticity and family life. It aids the memory, but can encourage possessiveness.

The New Moon in Leo gives self-confidence and some arrogance. This the time to show off and bask in the admiration of others.

The New Moon in Virgo is diligent and dutiful, giving a readiness to serve and a precision in decision-making.

The New Moon in Libra encourages diplomacy and tact. An emotional balancing act can be brought to a successful compromise.

The New Moon in Scorpio is a time of endings and new beginnings. Secrets may be revealed and long-held obsessions come to the surface.

The New Moon in Sagittarius promotes travel and anything that widens the experience of life. A time of optimism and luck.

The New Moon in Capricorn favours the ambitious and determined. Cool logic will win out over emotional considerations.

The New Moon in Aquarius makes one independent and rebellious. Humanitarian and progressive issues will predominate now.

The New Moon in Pisces aids the imagination and the deeper, more spiritual self. On a practical level, this time may be confusing.

THE NEW MOON IN THE HOUSES

The New Moon in the first house brings the start of some wonderful personal opportunities. New experiences await you, so be brave and embrace the novel. Now is a good time to change or spruce up your image.

The New Moon in the second house brings the start of prosperity. There will be the chance to increase your income, add to your savings or plan for your financial future.

The New Moon in the third house is a thoughtful time. Think deeply about where you want to go and what you want to achieve. Don't be afraid to take a calculated risk. Travel is well-starred, as are any educational ventures.

The New Moon in the fourth house puts the accent on your domestic and family life. This is a good time to move home or to reorganize your living arrangements. You may come to terms with issues from your past.

The New Moon in the fifth house urges you to use your innate talents to the full. This is the time for creativity, so try your hand at painting a masterpiece, writing a bestseller or becoming a cordon bleu chef. This is also a good time to conceive.

The New Moon in the sixth house may offer a new job, promotion or a beneficial change in your circumstances. This New Moon offers a chance of health improvements and renewed vitality.

The New Moon in the seventh house puts the focus on committed relationships. This is a good time for romance to flourish. Engagements, weddings and happy meetings are forecast. It's also a time to bury the hatchet.

The New Moon in the eighth house is steamy, physical and sensual, and a time of wild infatuation for some. For others a serious look at finances, investments and insurance wouldn't be a bad idea.

The New Moon in the ninth house opens up your horizons. Travel, explore fascinating new locales and prepare to abandon preconceptions. Those in the legal professions or in higher education will do very well.

'A ship, an isle, a sickle moon –
With few but with how
splendid stars
The mirrors of the sea
are strewn
Between their silver bars.'

James Elroy Flecker,
An Ship, an Isle, a Sickle Moon

'The gem Moonstone is considered to be a charm helpful in reconciling lovers.'

The New Moon in the tenth house urges you to reach for the sky, cut out the middle man and go right to the top. Seize the initiative and you could do your career a lot of good. This is a time for the ambitious.

The New Moon in the eleventh house shows that this is the time to do something positive to fulfil your hopes and dreams. The most unlikely wish can come true when this New Moon shines.

The New Moon in the twelfth house opens the psychic doorways of your perception. Expect precognitive dreams and stunning intuitive insights. Your kindness and generosity will now be appreciated.

THE FULL MOON

THE FULL MOON IN THE SIGNS

Whereas the New Moon can provide opportunities, the Full Moon presents challenges and shows the results of previous actions.

The Full Moon in Aries brings self-doubt and a need to question impulsive motives.

The Full Moon in Taurus makes you extra-possessive, almost to the point of obsession. Questions of ownership arise.

The Full Moon in Gemini may find you talking yourself into trouble. If in doubt, keep silent.

The Full Moon in Cancer is powerfully emotional and nostalgic. Old issues may haunt you now.

The Full Moon in Leo puts you in a playful mood even if there is serious work to be done.

The Full Moon in Virgo could make a martyr of you. Think about your own interests, too.

The Full Moon in Libra will reduce your decision-making ability. You will desperately want to please.

The Full Moon in Scorpio makes your extra-secretive, suspicious and very sensitive to any hint of criticism.

The Full Moon in Sagittarius opens your eyes to wonderful potentials, but takes your mind from pressing duties.

The Full Moon in Capricorn may make you dissatisfied with your lot and resentful of those who seem to be doing better than you.

The Full Moon in Aquarius makes you fiercely, if not aggressively, independent, eccentric and rebellious.

The Full Moon in Pisces makes you extra-sensitive to the moods and feelings of others. A hint of psychic awareness can be expected.

THE FULL MOON IN THE HOUSES

The Full Moon in the first house brings tension into a relationship. This could cause you to doubt yourself. You may be criticized or undermined in some way.

The Full Moon in the second house may bring a cash-flow crisis. Your confidence may be undermined by an embarrassing secret being revealed.

The Full Moon in the third house challenges your understanding. You may feel the need to improve qualifications or expand your capabilities in some way.

The Full Moon in the fourth house could bring tension into the domestic scene. You could experience career problems. You may try to cope with too much at once.

The Full Moon in the fifth house give impetus to creativity and romantic urges. However, patience and restraint at this time may lead to frustration.

The Full Moon in the sixth house shows it is time to abandon bad habits. Take notice of the state of your health. You may need to employ a workman at short notice.

The Full Moon in the seventh house brings relationship problems to the fore. Dealing with these may be emotionally trying, but deal with them you must.

The Full Moon in the eighth house either puts the spotlight on financial dealings or on your intimate sex life. Beware of hysteria or over-reaction to anything.

The Full Moon in the ninth house shows restlessness. You'll want more out of life, but may not be able to see a way of escaping your particular rut.

LUNAR LEGEND

The first ten days after a New Moon are considered portentous.

THE FIRST DAY is good to begin new ventures, but if you fall ill on this day the malady will last a long time. Children born at a New Moon will live long and prosper.

THE SECOND DAY gives excellent prospects for sales people. In fact, it is a good time to buy or sell anything. It is auspicious for sea voyages, for farmers to plough and for seeds to be sown. Children born on this day be very persuasive.

THE THIRD DAY is an ominous one, so care should be taken. Double-dealers and criminals fare worst because they are likely to be caught. Children born now may be sickly.

THE FOURTH DAY is good for the start of any construction work. All domestic affairs, and those connected with houses and buildings generally will be successful. Children born on this day will be subtle and may favour politics.

THE FIFTH DAY reveals the weather pattern for the rest of the month. It is an excellent time for the conception of a child to occur. Children born on this day will possess great sensitivity and be very creative.

THE SIXTH DAY is most auspicious for those who hunt or fish, since the haul will be good. Children born on this day will be enterprising and fond of the outdoor life.

THE SEVENTH DAY is the best for affairs of the heart to flourish. Take note of anyone you meet on this day, for romance is in the air. Children born now will be kind and loving.

THE EIGHTH DAY is a gloomy one for health matters and bodes ill for anyone who contracts an ailment on this day. Children born now will have a leaning towards the medical profession.

THE NINTH DAY'S influence warns of madness if one should allow the light of the Moon to fall on one's face while asleep. Even if Moon-madness is avoided, a perpetual look of fear may be left on the features. Children born on this day will be hard to understand.

THE TENTH DAY is good for travel and explorations of any kind. Children born on this day will be restless and journey far.

The Full Moon in the tenth house brings challenges in the career – either a sudden breakthrough in a static work situation or a resentment of authority.

The Full Moon in the eleventh house brings irritations with friends and colleagues. Younger people could prove troublesome and stretch your patience.

The Full Moon in the twelfth house shows the need to relax, to only do those things which absolutely must be done. Analyze your actions and options now.

·

ECLIPSES

The cycle of the Earth, Moon and Sun is a complex affair. It is when these three bodies come into perfect alignment at a New or Full Moon that an eclipse will occur.

When the Moon is new it may pass directly in front of the Sun. This is called a solar eclipse because the Sun's light will be temporarily blocked by the mass of the Moon itself. The eclipse may be total, covering the Sun completely for up to seven-and-half minutes, during which time birds cease their song, the air becomes chilly and a sort of ominous hush descends. The most remarkable sight is the corona or halo of the Sun visible around the dark face of the Moon. A partial eclipse is not so eerie because the light of the Sun remains strong even though a chunk of the brilliant orb is covered. On the other hand, an eclipse occurring at the time of a Full Moon is a lunar eclipse because the Sun is on the other side of the Earth as it were, and it is the Earth's shadow that will darken the Moon. This shadow is called the umbra, and it passes across the face of the Moon causing it to go through all its phases in several hours.

Of course because the Moon is so much smaller than the Earth, roughly one-sixth of its size, an eclipse will only be visible by someone in the path of the shadow. In August 1999 the people of Europe were treated to a spectacular total solar eclipse which darkened the sky from Cornwall in South-West England to Romania and, indeed, well into Asia.

'On a Full Moon use rosehips, pomegranate, orange peel, cinnamon and cloves.'

Astrologically speaking, eclipses have generally been regarded with dread, presaging nothing but disaster. However, we now know that eclipses occur according to a complex cycle of planetary and lunar movements and there are likely to be at least three sets of solar and lunar eclipses each year. The horror of the seemingly unnatural transformation of day into night which happens at a solar eclipse is thankfully a thing of the past as we have learned to appreciate one of nature's grandest spectacles.

Modern astrological thinking holds that eclipses signify a major turning point, but do not point to doom, death and destruction. If you look at the eclipse tables you may well find that a significant date in your own life has been signposted by a lunar or solar eclipse.

●

Your Lunar Talisman

A lunar talisman is a symbol of the moon, such as a moon-shaped pendant or moonstone, with magical or protective powers. This may be worn around your neck or your wrist or just kept as an ornament to bring a little lunar magic into your life.

To empower your talisman, light a white candle and sit quietly. The best time for a personal wish is the night of the New Moon. If, however, the wish is for someone else then the night of the Full Moon is the right one.

Clear your thoughts while holding your talisman in both hands. If there is a particular wish that you have in mind, think of this now. It will help to focus your desire if you write this down on a plain white piece of paper. It may be that you hope to increase your income, fulfil a long-held ambition, or find a lover. This wish can be impressed by your will and your mind into the unique talisman. However, do not wish for negative things or hope for bad luck to fall on others because such malevolent thoughts can only rebound on the sender.

If you find it helps you to focus your wish, a prayer or mantra may be spoken out loud. You can compose a prayer yourself or choose a favourite piece of poetry.

When you feel that you have impressed your wishes on the talisman, leave it on a windowsill where it will be bathed in the rays of the Moon. Now take the piece of paper on which you have written your wish and carefully burn it in the candle flame (remember that safety is paramount, so don't set fire to the curtains or yourself while you are doing it). Now allow the candle to burn down and to extinguish itself naturally.

Finally, the next morning, gather up the remains of the candle, and particularly the charred bits of paper, and throw them into running water. Leave the talisman on the windowsill for one lunar cycle of 28 days, so that it is thoroughly bathed in the Moon's essence. You may now wear or keep your unique talisman with confidence that it will help to fulfil your wishes. Be patient, the talisman won't work in five minutes, but as time goes on you will find that your hopes and desires will come true.

•

CREATING MOON HOROSCOPES

THE PROGRESSED MOON

A progression of the Moon is a mathematical calculation of the movement of the Moon by the ratio of one day for one year. In fact, astrologers often call this kind of progression day-for-a-year-progressions. If this confuses you, don't worry because all will shortly be made clear.

When it comes to predictive astrology, there are a variety of techniques that astrologers can use. Two simple ones that don't require a computer or a boffin to work out are the progressions and the transits. In this chapter, we will show you how to progress the Moon to any period in your life – past, present or future – and how to interpret the progressed Moon once you have worked it out.

The Moon takes about 27 years to progress through all the signs of the zodiac and come back to where it was when you were born. This time scale varies a little because the progressions are not entirely even, but 27 years is a good rough guide. The Moon can take anything from two to three years to progress through each sign of the zodiac with an average of around two-and-a-half years per sign. This means that a whole block of your life can be influenced by the Moon's journey through a particular part of the sky. Just to give you one example of what this means, a progression through the 'relationship' signs of Libra and Scorpio can change your relationship situation. This doesn't mean that you are bound to break up relationships and make new ones – although you could do just that. What it does mean is that something will occur that changes the structure of your personal relationships. If a couple decided to have a baby, that would change the structure of their relationship in a pleasant way, and that could well occur when the Moon is progressing through these two signs – among many other possibilities.

Here is another example, when your Moon progresses through the workaholic sign of Capricorn, you can be sure that life is serious, and that you are fulfilling your career ambitions to the hilt. If you are ever going to make it big, this is one of the times when you have the chance of doing so. However, at the end of this progression, the Moon moves on to the 'breakout' sign of Aquarius and you can expect all kinds of havoc to occur. You may change your job, move house, change your partner for a new one, and be filled with original and rather impractical ideas. If you are really unlucky, you can lose all that you gained in material wealth during the stately Capricorn progression. You may then have to wait several years until the Moon has passed through Aquarius, Pisces, Aries and enters the sign of Taurus before you get your life together again and your money back!

While the Moon is progressing through the signs of the zodiac it is also progressing through your astrological houses, but let us take this a step at a time and first discover how you find which sign your Progressed Moon is in at any one time and leave the houses for later.

*'In Buddhist tradition the Moon
represents peace, serenity and beauty.
Full and New Moons are times of strength
and spiritual power.'*

THE METHOD

By now you will have used the charts on pp. 18–19 (Finding your Moon Sign) to discover the sign the Moon was in on your birthday. Once I have explained the progression system, you will use it in exactly the same way to find your Progressed Moon.

Note down your birthday on a piece of paper, then simply count ahead one day for every year of your life. For instance, if you want to know what life will be like when you are 29 years old, you simply count forwards 29 days from your birthdate and make a note of the new date.

EXAMPLE

If you were born on 10 April and you are now aged 20, count forwards 20 days to look up 30 April in the charts on pp. 18–19. If you are 21, 1 May would be the calculation date.

If you were born on 10 April 1986, according to the charts on pp. 18–19 (Finding your Moon Sign), this would put the Moon at the time of your birth in the sign of Taurus. If you want to find the Progressed Moon for when you are 18, add 18 days to your birth date, which will bring you to 28 April. According to the chart, the Moon will occupy the sign of Capricorn. At the age of 21 the significant date will be 1 May, so the Moon will then occupy the sign of Aquarius.

If you continue this process and calculate the Progressed Moon for the age of 70 or even 100, the method remains the same. At 70 the Moon will occupy Pisces, while on your 100th birthday it will be in the sign of Taurus.

Remember that as well as being placed in a sign of the zodiac, the Moon will also be in a particular house, so assuming that the Moon was in the House of Image at birth, it will have progressed to Capricorn and the House of Relationships by the time the subject is 18, to the House of Sex at 21, to Pisces and the House of Spirituality at 70, and finally to the House of Friendships at 100 years.

Remember that your natal or 'birth' Moon remains a fixed point on your personal chart. The Progressed Moon may make an aspect to it, or to the Sun or the ascendant as it 'progresses' through the zodiac during your lifetime.

If you want to know what life was like when you were 17, you count forwards 17 days from your birthday – and if you want to know what life will be like when you are 78, you count forwards 78 days from your birthday. That's all there is to it!

Once you have done this, turn to the charts on pp. 18–19, find out where the Moon is on the new date and you will soon see which sign your Progressed Moon is in during the year that you wish to examine.

Note: There are a couple of things to take into account. The first is that if you were born some time in February, your counting may cross from February into March. February contains 28 days except for leap years in which case you will have to remember that the 29th of February adds an extra day. 1960 was a leap year, so you might have to work backwards or forwards in four-year increments to see whether your year of birth was also a leap year. For example, 1956, 1960, 1964, 1968, 1972 etc.

The second thing to be aware of is that if your birthday is very late in the year and you want to look at your prospects for a particular year – say 2003 for example – you will need to bear the late birthday in mind. For example, if you were born on the 22 November 1980, you will only be 22 years old during most of 2003, so you will need to count forwards only 22 days to give you a flavour of most of the year 2003.

Once you have gone through the technique a couple of times, this will all fall into place. At worst, you can read through the interpretations for the Progressed Moon moving through two signs, say starting off in Taurus and then progressing to Gemini.

●

THE PROGRESSED MOON THROUGH THE SIGNS

AN ARIES PROGRESSION

The Moon progressing into Aries shows that the lesson you have to learn in this period of your life is one of courage. This is no time to take a back seat. Be egotistical, stand up for yourself and what you believe in. You may have periodic outbursts of anger, which is a subtle lunar way of telling you that you are not burning off enough excess energy. Herein lies the danger of the Moon progressing through fiery Aries. Endeavour to control misdirected fury or you may be counting the cost in guilt for a long time to come. The house placement of the Progressed Moon will show you the cause to fight for.

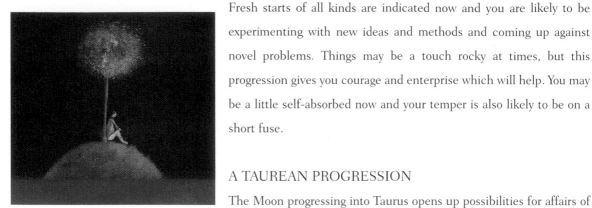

Fresh starts of all kinds are indicated now and you are likely to be experimenting with new ideas and methods and coming up against novel problems. Things may be a touch rocky at times, but this progression gives you courage and enterprise which will help. You may be a little self-absorbed now and your temper is also likely to be on a short fuse.

A TAUREAN PROGRESSION

The Moon progressing into Taurus opens up possibilities for affairs of the heart. You need some tranquility in your life now that the warfare of the last two and a half years is over. Get closer to nature, take up gardening, cultivate something that is yours alone. On the subject of cultivation, your finances need some attention, too. This is the time for savings plans and a sound investment policy. You may gain a little weight with the Moon progressing here, but that is nothing to worry about – it merely shows a new contentment in life. Past efforts are rewarded with the Moon here.

Issues of land, property and ownership could arise during this progression, either because you are establishing yourself or, less happily, because you are splitting up from someone and sorting out who should have what. This can be a time of growth, either in personal terms or in business and related matters. Money issues become important during this progression.

A GEMINI PROGRESSION

The Moon progressing into Gemini urges you to get out and about. The inflexible nature of the last two and a half years must be put aside now as you learn to cope with the new. Read widely; go to the movies, museums and galleries; travel as much as you can because the world has so much to offer someone with an open mind. Remember childlike curiosity and amazement? Well, you can rediscover them now. Let your imagination roam free and talk, talk, talk… to anyone who will listen. Communication and a creative expression of your personality through speaking and writing will lead you to many exciting encounters.

Your perceptions will develop now and you will be keeping a sharp eye on all that is going on around you. You might feel an urge to educate yourself or to gain experience in the fields of new technology. You are probably analyzing your feelings and also those of your loved ones, so you may be a little cool towards lovers during this progression.

A CANCERIAN PROGRESSION

The Moon progressing into Cancer is very important since the Moon traditionally has the greatest influence on this sign. Your imagination will be at its peak in this two-and-a-half-year period. Let your deepest fantasies come to the forefront of your mind. Accept that your emotional self needs some attention. This is a time to draw into yourself and to learn who you are emotionally. The main issue of this period is one of security. If you feel safe all will be well, but if not, your main efforts should be directed to providing yourself with the stability and comfort that you yearn for.

At best, you will feel contented and settled during this progression, but at worst your moods will be hard to control and to understand at times. You may even find your moods changing along with the phase of the Moon or with the tides. You will want to spend more time with the family and you may move house. Issues of motherhood could become important now.

A LEO PROGRESSION

The Moon progressing into Leo lets drama into your life. There is nothing wrong in this, especially if you are the type to place yourself firmly centre stage and in the spotlight. If you are not, it may be time to learn to take a more prominent role. Don't worry that you may seem self-centred – there's a time and a place for everything, and this is it! Be bold, be brash and ignore all criticism. You will have fun, even if there is a touch of embarrassment along the way (hopefully this will mature into wisdom before long). Remind yourself that others don't seem to have any trouble while being ruled by their egos, so why should you?

Romance, love affairs and matters of the heart rise to the surface now. If you are looking for love, this is when you might find it. Children and young people will feature strongly in your life now. If you are into creative or enterprising jobs or hobbies, these will receive a real boost.

'The moving moon went
up the sky,
And nowhere did abide:
Softly she was going up,
And a star or two
beside.'

S. T. Coleridge,
The Ancient Mariner, Pt III

A VIRGOAN PROGRESSION

The Moon progressing into Virgo is a reverse of the last two and a half years. Now your faults and foibles are shown up harshly under your critical gaze. Nothing you do will seem good enough or worthwhile. You will be keenly aware of the needs of others and will feel a strong urge to help in any way you can, even to the extent of becoming something of a martyr. If this sounds terrible, don't worry. The truth is that you will be able to truly judge your faults and advantages against those of everyone else. Be honest with yourself, because you have nothing to be ashamed of and you are doing better than most.

During this progression, you will become keen to improve your health and appearance, so diet and exercise might become important. Work will take up more of your time and if you are looking for promotion or a change of job, this is when you should go for it. You may feel a strange urge to tidy yourself or your life up, so you could find yourself throwing aside material things or even people you no longer need.

A LIBRAN PROGRESSION

The Moon progressing into Libra will bring new people into your life. Friendships which may or may not develop into strong emotional attachments are a major feature for the next two and a half years.

You may not feel very independent and may need someone to hold your hand or give you the support you crave. You may become more vain now as you give in to the urge to transform your appearance, and you constantly check on how good you look. Beauty, aesthetics, social interaction and a high standard of life are the key concepts for the Moon progressing through Libra.

Romance is in the air, with the Moon entering the relationship area of your life. If you are single, you may date more than usual, but don't expect the first person you try out to be the one you end up with. You may have to kiss a few frogs along the way! Business may bring new people into your life and you may start an important partnership at some point.

A SCORPIO PROGRESSION

The Moon progressing into Scorpio begins a very serious period in your life. Although there will be some light-hearted moments, the main thrust of the next two and a half years will be deep and brooding. You will look into the depths of your soul and begin a phase of inner confrontation which may spill over into your daily life. This is the most psychologically challenging of the Moon's progressions, bringing an awareness of mortality and the implications of close attachments to others. Be brave, face your deepest fears and you will find that they weren't so terrifying after all. You will emerge on the other side stronger and more capable.

This progression is crucial for relationships because Scorpio rules uniting and parting. Serious changes in your relationship status are possible now. The way others see you and the way they value you and your work is an important factor in your life during this progression.

A SAGITTARIAN PROGRESSION

The Moon progressing into Sagittarius casts serious concerns aside as you enter a prolonged period of exuberance and freedom. You are likely to resent any restrictions placed upon you and ditch them as swiftly as possible. All the soul-searching is over, and you may feel stronger and more self-willed, with a hunger to experience everything that life has to offer. Grab every opportunity that comes along – there will be a lot of them. Luck is on your side so be daring, change those things you don't like, and revel in the confidence that you are the sole owner of your life and can finally do what you want.

Freedom is the name of the game here, and you may try to disentangle yourself from ties that bind. You may want the freedom to come and go as you please, but most of all you will want to explore your deepest beliefs and to work out what you really want to achieve. You will

'It is best to cut hair and fingernails when the Moon is waning because they will grow back more slowly.'

want to explore what the world has to offer, whether through travel or education. Legal matters may become important during this progression.

A CAPRICORN PROGRESSION

The Moon progressing into Capricorn adds the elements of self-discipline and ambition to the exuberant freedom of the last two and a half years. You will be in a mood to put everything you have learned to good use, to accomplish something worthwhile and, for some, to reach the top of the career ladder. You can, and will, do it in this lunar period, but since the Moon governs feelings, you must remember to voice your emotions and not get too obsessed with worldly achievement. Otherwise you will experience loneliness as you exclude all those who can't be a part of your upward mobility.

You may look the same on the outside, but a good deal of ambition is now bubbling away under the surface. If you are going to make it big in your career, it is likely to be during this progression. You may go through a rough patch or time of struggle, but you will learn more about life and about yourself during this time than when life is easy.

AN AQUARIAN PROGRESSION

The Moon progressing into Aquarius brings back your independence in vast quantities. It may add to your reputation for eccentricity too, since you will be all too happy to bend or even break the rules that constrain you. This is a period when you should experiment with actions and ideas. Don't be afraid of disapproval; your life is more important than any negative views

held by anyone else. Your true hopes and wishes will emerge now, and you should turn your efforts towards ensuring that they don't just remain pipe dreams. This is a rebellious influence for many, but any disruptions will be worth the shock waves.

The chances are that you will finish this progression living in a different way than you did at the start. You may move house, change career, meet a new partner or leave an old one, or simply change your outlook. Original thinking and inventive ideas characterize this progression, as does kicking over the traces.

A PISCEAN PROGRESSION

The Moon progressing into Pisces brings a sense of unreality to your life. You may feel that the real world isn't so real after all and that true enlightenment exists within your dreams. Your psychic nature will be enhanced by this two-and-a-half-year period because Pisces is the most mystical of all the signs. You will see the subtle links between everything: people, places, cars, animals, nature itself... You name it and you will find the connections with something else. This gentle, contemplative side to your character will attract the right people to you in this most sensitive and caring of times.

'Slowly, silently, now the moon Walks the night in her silver shoon.'

Walter De La Mare, *Silver*

You are likely to meet up with more kindness and affection than usual during this progression, and your own attitude will become gentler as well. Your emotions will become stronger and you will feel deeply about people and things, even if you are normally fairly cold-hearted. You will feel restless and you could have an urge to travel more.

●

THE PROGRESSED MOON THROUGH THE HOUSES

Now that we have looked at the Progressed Moon through the signs, let us see what happens to the astrological houses. Again, this sounds complicated, but it is easy to work out and to understand by following the instructions step by step. If you haven't already done so, use the wheel in the pocket at the back of the book to work out your rising sign. (If you don't know your exact time of birth, you won't be able to go any further with this chapter.)

Next, look at the wheel and see the layout of the houses. They run from 1 to 12 round the wheel from your rising sign. For example, Gemini rising is the first house, with Cancer being the second, Leo the third and so on.

Now check out the house that your Progressed Moon is in.

THE MOON PROGRESSING INTO THE HOUSE OF IMAGE

This period brings a sense of newness, characterized by childlike feelings of wonder and curiosity. A fresh cycle of life is beginning, and everything that is undertaken now will develop as the Moon progresses through all the succeeding houses. You may feel somewhat uncertain at this time and express this anxiety as an obsession with your physical appearance. Often you will feel your way through difficulties rather than carefully working out each step. It is important that you don't allow anyone else to hold you back or keep you from making your own mistakes and learning by them.

The movement of the Moon into the House of Image brings emotions to the surface for a while. You may feel particularly good about life now and it is probably a good idea to tell your friends and loved ones how much they mean to you. Your mood is enterprising and you will be ready to try out new methods of doing things.

> ## 'Lunar creatures are the crab, lobster, tortoise, owl, otter, cuckoo and frog.'

THE MOON PROGRESSING INTO THE HOUSE OF WEALTH

Now is the time to ask yourself 'Can you finish what you have started?' You may feel uncertain about your future initially, but this will develop into a tough determination. Issues concerning your personal value system will emerge now. You will feel the need to build up your financial resources as a cure for insecurities. The monetary angle of this house is a long-term venture, and you should not expect sudden windfalls or gifts of unearned income. On the contrary, solid, steady effort is required to make your economic desires a reality.

While the Moon is in the House of Wealth it is time to sit back and reassess how far you have come and what you have achieved materially. It might be worth considering where you were when you started and how much further you think you can go.

THE MOON PROGRESSING INTO THE HOUSE OF TRAVEL

This will jolt you out of a rut and open your eyes to new horizons, locations and ideas you hadn't entertained before. You will now be restless and endlessly curious, seeking knowledge through conversations as well as more formal areas of learning. Your brothers, sisters or friends and relatives of your own generation will have a strong influence now, and you may renew close relationships that had drifted apart. Often, the restlessness of the Moon progressing through this house urges the purchase of a new vehicle.

The emphasis will be on communication with others for a while. Whether this means phoning, writing, faxing, emailing etc., or learning to communicate in a wider sense, your skills will need to be brushed up, even if this only means learning how to express your feelings and to listen to what others have to say to you.

THE MOON PROGRESSING INTO THE HOUSE OF HOME

This progression is almost like coming home, since this is the house with more lunar associations than any other. It is time to take stock of yourself, your surroundings and the state of your family. Issues from your childhood may resurface, and this is the time to deal with them, so put away old hurt and bruised egos, forgive and forget – if possible. They say that truth will come out in the end, and truth, no matter how painful, will make its presence felt now.

'Flowers associated with the Moon are acanthus, lotus (water lily) and wild flowers.'

You will find yourself looking backwards in some way during this phase, either with fond memories or in order to dig down and sort out psychological problems that have arisen from the past. You will want to settle down somewhere and have a home, or even just a room within a house, that you can call your own.

THE MOON PROGRESSING INTO THE HOUSE OF PLEASURE

This progression can be a tempestuous influence, spurring you on to whirlwind affairs, a fast-paced extravaganza of fun and frolics. However, this isn't the whole story. This house also relates to children and creativity. If you were hoping for a baby, this Progressed Moon may well bring this about. In fact, any issues involving your offspring or those who fulfil the role of offspring become very important now. Your creative potential should be given an airing. If you have ever had a desire to write a bestseller or paint a masterpiece, have a go now.

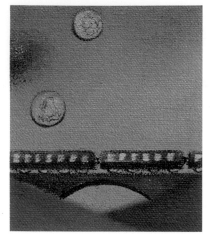

Dealings with children or young people will be an important issue during this progression. You may feel quite light-hearted at times due to the youthful influence around you. Creative ventures will get off the ground now, but despite being busy you will find time to relax. There is a hint of flirtation and love in the air.

THE MOON PROGRESSING INTO THE HOUSE OF HEALTH

This period will affect your habits, daily routine, working life, and any dealings you have with workmen or anyone whom you pay for a service. The Moon here is unrelenting. It is nose-to-the-grindstone time with very little leisure to enjoy yourself. You may be taken down a peg or two, but that is just to teach you a little humility, not to humiliate you. You will still have to stand up for your rights, but the difference is that you may have to stand up for the rights of others as well.

This lunar progression means that you must concentrate on your work and also on your physical health. The message here is to get your career on-track and also to automate household chores as far as possible so that you don't wear yourself out. Stress may be a factor in health problems at this time.

THE MOON PROGRESSING INTO THE HOUSE OF RELATIONSHIPS

This progression works out the difference between 'fuzzy', rather ambiguous emotional links and those that will stand the test of time. This progression is notoriously hard on marriages because it will test your commitment again and again over two and a half years. The only secure way through this troublesome time is to communicate openly with your partner. If this is not possible, perhaps he or she is not the one for you. At least all the cards will be on the table, for good or ill – actually it is good, even though you might not feel that way at the time.

With all the challenges you have had to face out in the world, it is easy to forget that you have a personal life too. If you are in a long-standing relationship, remember to give some time and attention to your lover. If you are looking for someone new to share your life with, date now, but don't expect to find the right person immediately.

THE MOON PROGRESSING INTO THE HOUSE OF SEX

This highlights your inner drives. You may find that you have passions that you didn't know existed, that have been buried under tons of repression. Well, it is now time to let some of that guilt and foreboding go. Free up a little, admit to a foible or two. It's not the end of the world, and you may well find a tremendous commitment to someone special once you get rid of those hang-ups. Your instincts will be powerful in this period, possibly at the expense of the intellect. There's nothing wrong in that, so be an animal and let your hair down.

Issues relating to partnerships are coming to the surface now and you may come to the conclusion that the person you are seeing is the one you want to spend the rest of your life with. Alternatively, you may decide that the relationship you are in is no longer fulfilling your needs and this may lead you to call a halt to it. Joint finances will need to be looked into as well.

THE MOON PROGRESSING INTO THE HOUSE OF SPIRITUALITY

This is the start of a life-changing journey, both inside your own head and outside in the big wide world. You may come to the startling realization that life is for the living, so don't let petty restrictions and boring rules hold you back. The gates of freedom are thrown wide, and it won't take much to make you head off to the high sierras of adventure. Your inner journey leads you to speculate on the unbelievable possibilities of the universe. You may take up higher education to expand your experience.

You may begin to feel that your life is too restricted, and decide to expand your horizons, perhaps by travelling, improving your knowledge and education or by doing something new. What is certain is that you won't stay in your rut for much longer. Legal matters and even religion and belief may become important to you now.

THE MOON PROGRESSING INTO THE HOUSE OF CAREER

This progression is like a starting pistol for your ambitions. You may feel the need to change your job, to take up new challenges and to rise to

'He made an instrument
to know
If the moon shine at
full or no.'

Samuel Butler, *Hudibras*

the top of the heap. Your professional star is rising, so grit your teeth and go with it. You will come over as an extremely capable and efficient person as you learn about the amazing things that you can actually accomplish. Your status too becomes a pressing issue now. You will ask yourself, 'Am I getting the respect I deserve?' That question provides a spur to proving yourself.

You are becoming more conscious of your public image now and crave admiration and respect. You will have to work hard to achieve this, but if you put in the effort, you will be rewarded. During this progression, you will work hard and so will feel quite tired for much of the time.

THE MOON PROGRESSING INTO THE HOUSE OF FRIENDSHIPS

Now all your social interactions, clubs, societies and affiliations, as well as your hopes, wishes and dreams, are highlighted. Your humanitarian instincts come to the fore, as well as a strong desire to unite with others who share your values and ideals. However, you will be startlingly independent-minded, so finding the right group to join may be a problem initially. Even so, many of your desires for yourself and the world at large will now be clarified. So don't be shy, go out there and make a difference.

Friends and acquaintances become important to you now and you could find yourself becoming close to a different group of people. Life might not be as stable as usual and you may move house, change your job or experience changes in your relationships.

THE MOON PROGRESSING INTO THE HOUSE OF SECRETS

Some deep thinking is in order now. You may feel that a wonderful period is drawing to a close, or alternatively you might just be glad to see the back of this hectic time. Either way, you'll be left to your own devices for a while. You may have work to do which restricts you in some way. You won't feel as sociable as in the past, but this is nothing to worry about. Just relax and don't take on anything too pressurized. Let go of some of your responsibilities and explore the more mystical you. You may have precognitive dreams.

You might be almost psychic at times, and will be aware of emotional undercurrents. You will be able to read others like open books. However, you may also be affected by other people's anxieties, so avoid disturbing people or influences.

CREATING YOUR OWN HOROSCOPE

USING TRANSITS FOR DAILY HOROSCOPES

Transits make up the type of horoscopes you see in the newspapers, but these are always confined to the Sun sign because that is all most people usually understand. Transits are also used by professional astrologers who give personal consultations where the astrologer has the whole of a person's birthchart to play with. A good consultant astrologer will also use progressions, Solar returns and probably other techniques that are not included in this book.

Here we take a middle road by showing you the kind of energy that everybody on the Earth can feel when the transiting Moon moves through the signs of the zodiac, and then the kind of energy that only you and those who share your rising sign can feel as the transiting Moon moves through the houses of your horoscope.

THE METHOD

The Moon takes about two and a half days to transit through a sign and it takes 28 days to move round the Earth and thus through all 12 signs of the zodiac.

Working out the transiting Moon's position at any time is extremely easy. Just as you used the charts on pp. 18–19 (Finding Your Moon Sign) to work out where the Moon was on the day you were born, you use the chart in exactly the same way to discover the transiting Moon's position on any day that you want to examine. If you want to see where it is today, simply look it up on the chart as if today was someone's date of birth. If you want to see what a specific date later in the year will be like, just use that date. The same goes for any date up to the year 2010. If you want to track back to a day in your past, you can do so – just use the chart as instructed for finding the any date of birth. It's that easy! See box on p.106 for example.

THE TRANSITS OF THE MOON THROUGH THE SIGNS

Aries – This transit means that it is time to take the initiative and get to grips with things now. This is no time to hide your light under a bushel.

EXAMPLE

If you were born on 2 September 1957 at 11pm, your rising sign is Gemini, the Sun is in Virgo in the House of Home, and the Moon is in Sagittarius in the House of Relationships, showing that you are practically minded and ambitious. Although you are sociable and have many friends, you are prepared to sacrifice a great deal for your home and family.

If you wanted to know the likelihood of business success on 3 June 2001, you would simply turn to the charts on pp. 18–19 (Finding your Moon Sign) and follow the same procedure you used for finding the Moon's position on your birthday.

The Moon will be in Scorpio on 3 June 2001, which equates to your House of Health. This house also relates to duty, employers and employees. There will be new opportunities at work and the chances of success in any business venture are extremely good. The Moon in Scorpio by transit is also important because it casts a good aspect to your rising sign of Gemini, which means that you will be showing yourself off to your best advantage.

On 3 June 2001 the Sun will be in Gemini, which is also your rising sign. This enhances your personality and makes you extra charming and outgoing. The transiting Sun casts a negative aspect to your natal Sun in Virgo, which shows that even though this is a good period you won't have things completely your own way.

Taurus – Now is a good time for undertaking practical or creative jobs. If you like music and dancing, take your lover out and boogie on down!

Gemini – This transit tells you to get down to all that correspondence, make phone calls and pop out to do errands or see friends. It's good to talk!

Cancer – It is time to concentrate on family and the domestic scene. You could contact your parents, for example, or cook something nice for dinner for your loved ones.

Leo – You are entitled to have some fun and this is the time in which to do so. If you have children, take them out somewhere nice.

Virgo – Chores have to be done and this is the time to do them. You may not have much fun for a day or two, but you will feel better for having got a few backed-up jobs out of the way.

Libra – This is either a time of love and harmony or else a time when you must fight for your rights – perhaps a bit of both. Other people will be an important factor now.

Scorpio – Your relationships with others will come under scrutiny during this transit, but try to avoid being manipulated by them. If you are in love, passions will fly high.

'Ah, Moon of my Delight who know'st no wane, The Moon of Heav'n is rising once again.'

Edward Fitzgerald,
The Ruba'iyat of Omar Khayyam

Sagittarius – Consider what you think is the right thing to do and don't allow others to influence you unduly. Give yourself some space from others now if you can.

Capricorn – Concentrate on details during this transit and don't leave things to chance. If you need to talk to someone in a position of authority, this is the time to do so.

Aquarius – During an Aquarius transit, you may feel like kicking over the traces or doing something completely different. Go on, take a chance on life – you never know where it will lead to!

Pisces – You may have to give your time and attention to others for a while now. Alternatively, you may spend some time completely alone.

THE TRANSITING MOON THROUGH THE HOUSES

This adds a complication to the system because you will need to know where each of your houses are. The following instructions will make things clear.

First, find your rising sign and treat this sign as your first house. (If you don't know your time of birth, you won't be able to take this any further.)

Using the Astrological Houses wheel, place your rising sign in the first house. The other houses will follow around the wheel in turn.

Check which sign the Moon is transiting on whatever date you want and see which house this is. For instance, if your rising sign is Cancer, this is your first house, so if the transiting Moon happens to be in Libra today, it will be crossing your fourth house. When you use the wheel, you will immediately see which house the transiting Moon is in on the day you wish to examine.

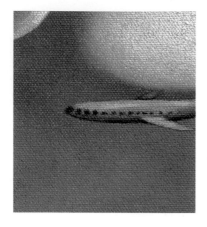

First House of Image – You will be conscious of your own inner feelings during this transit, and you might feel quite sensitive, vulnerable or emotional for a while. You may also feel quite restless.

Second House of Wealth – This is an excellent time to sort out your financial position and to make some much-needed adjustments. Look around for bargain buys.

Third House of Travel – During this transit, the emphasis will be on communication and learning. Someone may show you an easier or more efficient way of going about things.

Fourth House of Home – You may find yourself in a sentimental and nostalgic mood, so get out that old photo album or talk over the past with a family member. Also, this is a time to concentrate on home life.

Fifth House of Pleasure – They say that a little of what you fancy does you good, so get out and about and prepare to have some fun. If romance is in the air, this will be a good time for it.

Sixth House of Health – If you are off-colour, take some vitamins or do whatever else is necessary to put you right. Get down to work now as the chores can't be avoided.

Seventh House of Relationships – During this transit, you need to be spoiled and also to spoil your lover, so plan something nice for both of you now. Others will show that that they think a lot of you.

Eighth House of Sex – This is a time for serious consideration of your joint financial position – or indeed, any other important matter that involves others as well as yourself.

Ninth House of Spirituality – If you have relatives or other foreign contacts, this is a good time to get in touch with them. Legal, educational or even religious matters might become important now.

'If there are two New Moons in the same month then there will be a prolonged spell of bad weather.'

Tenth House of Career – You will need to put forward an image of probity and respectability for a while. You may be churning inside but your outer manner should be cool and in control.

Eleventh House of Friendships – You will have had enough of work for a while, so the social scene will take precedence now. If you are bored with the same old routine, try and find a different way of doing things.

Twelfth House of Secrets – A quiet time is indicated by this transit. You may have to pay some debts now or put something right that has gone wrong.

> *'The new moon hangs like an ivory bugle In the naked frosty blue.'*
>
> Edward Thomas,
> *The Penny Whistle*

'About once every three years there will be two Full Moons in a month. As this is quite rare, the second Full Moon is called a Blue Moon – from which the expression "once in a blue moon" comes.'

LUNAR ECLIPSE CYCLE FROM 2001 TO 2020

•

9 January 2001

5 July 2001

30 December 2001

26 May 2002

24 June 2002

20 November 2002

16 May 2003

9 November 2003

4 May 2004

28 October 2004

24 April 2005

17 October 2005

14 March 2006

7 September 2006

3 March 2007

28 August 2007

21 February 2008

1 August 2008

9 February 2009

7 July 2009

6 August 2009

31 December 2009

26 June 2010

21 December 2010

15 June 2011

10 December 2011

4 June 2012

28 November 2012

25 April 2013

25 May 2013

18 October 2013

15 April 2014

8 October 2014

4 April 2015

28 September 2015

23 March 2016

16 September 2016

11 February 2017

7 August 2017

31 January 2018

27 July 2018

21 January 2019

16 July 2019

10 January 2020

5 June 2020

30 November 2020

FURTHER READING

•

Astrology for Living, Sasha Fenton, Collins and Brown, 1999

Astrology...on the Move!, Sasha Fenton, Zambezi Publishing, 1998

Astrology – The Inner Eye, Elaine Smith, Capall Bann Publishing, 1997

Book of Prophecies, Jonathan Dee, Collins and Brown, 1999

House Book, The, Stephanie Camilleri, Llewellyn Publications, 1999

How to Read Your Star Signs, Sasha Fenton, Thorsons, 1998

Llewellyn's 2001 Moon Sign Book, Gloria Star, Llewellyn Publications, 2000

Moon Signs: The Key to Your Inner Life, Donna Cunningham,
    Ballantine Books, 1988

Venus and Mars, Robert Reid, Thorsons, 1998